WITCHCRAFT

The Modern Witch's Book of Herbs, Magick, and Dreams

Gerina Dunwich

A Citadel Press Book
Published by Carol Publishing Group

ALSO BY GERINA DUNWICH

Candlelight Spells
The Magick of Candle Burning
The Concise Lexicon of the Occult
Circle of Shadows (poetry)

Carol Publishing Group Edition, 1995

A Citadel Press Book
Published by Carol Publishing Group
Citadel Press is a registered trademark of Carol Communications, Inc.

Editorial Offices: 600 Madison Avenue, New York, NY 10022
Sales & Distribution Offices: 120 Enterprise Avenue, Secaucus, NJ 07094
In Canada: Canadian Manda Group, One Atlantic Avenue, Suite 105
Toronto, Ontario, M6K 3E7

Queries regarding rights and permissions should be addressed to:
Carol Publishing Group, 600 Madison Avenue, New York, NY 10022

Manufactured in the United States of America
15 14 13 12 11 10 9 8 7 6

Carol Publishing Group books are available at special discounts for bulk purchases, sales promotions, fund raising, or educational purposes. Special editions can also be created to specifications. For details contact: Special Sales Department, Carol Publishing Group, 120 Enterprise Ave., Secaucus, NJ 07094

Library of Congress Cataloging-in-Publication Data

Dunwich, Gerina
    Wicca craft: the book of herbs, magick, and dreams / Gerina Dunwich
      p.   cm.
    "A Citadel Press book."
    ISBN 0-8065-1238-5
    Includes bibliographical references and index.
    1. Magic. 2. Ritual. 3. Goddess religion. 4. Witchcraft.
    I. Title.
BF1623.R6D86   1991
133.4'3—dc20   91-7842
                                        CIP

I dedicate this book with loving gratitude to my Gemini lover and soul mate, Al B. Jackter; to Barbara Jacobson for all of her love, laughter, and friendship; and to my Mother, the stubborn (but loving) Taurus Bull.

THE CALL OF THE GODDESS

Awaken one, awaken all
and hear the voice of the Goddess call.
Rejoice! Rejoice!
Lift up your voice
and let our beautiful Mother Earth
be filled with magick, love, and mirth.
Let there be drink.
Let there be song.
Celebrate merrily all night long!

—from *Circle of Shadows*
by Gerina Dunwich

Contents

Introduction

Wicca (an alternative name for modern witchcraft) is a positive, shamanistic nature religion with two main deities honored and worshipped in Wiccan rites: the Goddess (the female aspect and a deity related to the ancient Mother Goddess in Her triple aspects of Maiden, Mother, and Crone) and Her consort, the Horned God (the male aspect). Their names vary from one Wiccan tradition to the next, and some traditions use different deity names in both their higher and lower degrees.

Wicca often includes the practice of various forms of white magick (usually for healing purposes or as a counter to negativity), as well as rites to attune oneself with the natural rhythm of life forces marked by the phases of the moon and the four seasons.

Wicca (which is also known as the "Craft of the Wise" or often just "The Craft") is considered by many to be both a monistic and pantheistic religion, and is part of the modern Pagan resurgence, or neo-Pagan movement, as many prefer to call it.

"Today, most people who define themselves as Pagans use the word as a general term for "native and natural religions, usually polytheistic, and their members." In simple terms, it is a positive, nature-based religion, preaching brotherly love and harmony with and respect for all life forms. It is very similar to Native American spirituality. Its origins are found in the early human development of religion: animistic deities gradually becoming redefined to become a main God or Goddess of all Nature. This God or Goddess—bearing different names at different times and in different places— can be found in nearly all of the world's historic religious systems. Paganism does not oppose nor deny any other religion. It is simply a pre-Christian faith.

Most Pagans seem to agree on many of these commonly held beliefs: (1) Divinity is immanent or internal, as well as transcendent or external. This is often expressed by the phrases "Thou Art God" and "Thou Art Goddess." (2) Divinity is just as likely to manifest itself as female. This has resulted in a large number of women being attracted to the faith and joining the clergy. (3) A multiplicity of gods and goddesses, whether as individual deities or as facets of one or a few archetypes. This leads to multi-valued logic systems and increased toler- ance towards other religions. (4) Respect and love of Nature as divine in Her own right. This makes ecological awareness and activity a religious duty. (5) Dissatisfaction with monolithic religious or- ganizations and distrust of would-be messiahs and gurus. This makes Pagans hard to organize, even "for their own good," and leads to constant muta- tion and growth in the movement. (6) The conviction that human beings were meant to live lives filled with joy, love, pleasure, and humor. The traditional Western concept of sin, guilt, and divine retribution are seen as misunderstandings of natural growth experiences. (7) A simple set of ethics and morality based on the avoidance of harm to other people. Some extend this to some or all living beings and the planet as a whole. (8) The knowledge that with proper training and intent, human minds and hearts are fully capable of performing all of the magic and miracles they are ever likely to need, through the use of natural psychic powers which everyone possesses. (9) The importance of acknowledging and celebrating the solar, lunar and other cycles of our lives. This has led to the investigation and revival of many ancient customs and the invention of some new ones. (10) A minimum of dogma and a maximum of eclecticism. That is to say, Pagans are reluctant to accept any idea without personally investigating it, and are willing to adopt and use any concept they find useful, regardless of its origins. (11) A strong faith in the ability of people to solve their own current problems on all levels, public and private. This leads to . . . (12) A strong commitment to personal and universal growth, evolution and balance. Pagans are expected to be making continuous efforts in these directions. (13) A belief that one can progress far towards achieving such growth, evolution and balance through the carefully planned alteration of one's consciousness, using both ancient and modern methods of aiding concentration, meditation, re-programming and ecstasy. (14) The knowledge that human interdependence implies community cooperation. Pagans are encouraged to use their talents to actively help each other as well as the community at large. (15) An awareness that if they are to achieve any of their goals, they must practice what they preach. This leads to a concern with making one's life-style consistent with one's proclaimed beliefs."(—From a handout for neighbors entitled **"What In Heaven's Name Is Going on Over There?"** copyright 1989 by the Center for Non-Traditional Religion, used with permission. For more information, see their Panegyria listing on page 189 in the Pagan Periodicals chapter.)

The Wiccan religion is made up of various sects (or "traditions") such as Gardnerian, Alexandrian, Dianic, Tanic, Georgian, ethnic Traditionalist, and so on. Many of the traditions were formed and introduced in the 1960s, and although their rituals, customs, myth cycles, and symbolisms may be different from one another, they all hold common principles of Craft law.

The main tenet of Wicca Craft is the Wiccan Rede, a simple and benevolent moral code that is as follows: AN IT HARM NONE, DO WHAT THOU WILT. Or, in other words, be free to do your own thing, provided that you in no way bring any harm upon anyone—including yourself. (The Wiccan Rede is extremely important to bear in mind before performing any magickal spells or rituals, especially those which may be considered unethical or of a manipulative nature.)

The Threefold Law (or Law of Three) is a karmic law of triple retribution which applies whenever you do something good or bad. For instance, if you use white magick (or positive energy) to do something good for somebody else, three times the good will come back to you in your lifetime. By the same token, if you use black magick (or negative energy) to bring harm unto others, the bad or "evil" will also return to you threefold in the same lifetime.

The followers of the Wiccan religion are called Wiccans or Witches. The word "Witch" applies to both male and female practitioners of the Craft. (Male witches or Wiccans are seldom, if ever, called Warlocks. The word "Warlock," which is considered an insult in most Wiccan circles, stems from the Old English WAER-LOGA, meaning an "oath-breaker," and was used derogatorily by the Christian Church as a name for a male witch.)

Although Witches are proud to be a part of the Craft, there are some who object strongly to the use of the term "Witch," feeling that the word possesses certain negative connotations and stirs up too many bizarre images and misconceptions in the minds of those who are unfamiliar with the Craft and perhaps a bit reluctant to accept that which they do not clearly understand.

As Wicca Craft is a Nature-oriented religion, most of its members are involved in one way or another with the ecology movement and current environmental issues.

Wiccans do not accept the arbitrary concept of innate sin or absolute evil, and they do not believe in a Heaven or a Hell, other than those which are one's own creations.

Wiccans do not practice any form of black magick or "evil," do not worship devils, demons, or any evil entities, and do not make attempts to convert members of other faiths to the Pagan way. Wiccans respect all other positive religions, and feel that a person must hear the "call of the Goddess" and truly desire within his or her own heart, without any outside influence or proselytization, to follow the Wiccan path.

Many Wiccans take on one or more secret names (also known as "Eke-names") to signify their spiritual rebirth and new life within the Wicca Craft. Eke-names are most sacred and are used only among brothers and sisters of the same path. When a Witch takes on a new name, she or he must be extremely careful to choose one that harmonizes in one way or another with numerological name-numbers, birth-numbers, or runic-numbers. A well-chosen name vibrates with that individual and directly links her or him to the Craft.

Many Wiccans work together in small groups which are called covens. The coven (which may consist of up to thirteen people) is lead by a High Priestess and/or a High Priest, and gathers together to worship the Goddess, work magick, and perform ceremonies at Sabbats and Esbats. The members of a coven are known as "coveners," and the place where a coven meets is called the "covenstead."

Wiccans who work on their own, either by personal choice or by circumstance, are called "solitary" Witches.

Wiccans celebrate eight Sabbats each year, marking transitions in the seasons. There are four major (or grand) Sabbats and four minor (or lesser) ones. The major Sabbats are: Candlemas, Beltane, Lammas, and Samhain. The minor Sabbats are: Spring Equinox, Summer Solstice, Autumn Equinox, and Winter Solstice. (These festival celebrations are covered in detail in Chapter Two.)

The Esbat is a monthly coven meeting held at least thirteen times a year during each full moon. At the Esbat, Wiccans exchange ideas, discuss problems, perform special rites, work magick and healing, and give thanks to the Goddess and the Horned God. A traditional "Cakes and Wine" or "Cakes and Ale" ceremony also takes place at the Esbat. During this ceremony,

consecrated food and refreshments are served, and coveners take time to relax and discuss important magickal
subjects. (The "Cakes and Wine" or "Cakes and Ale"
ceremony is a traditional custom whenever a Wiccan
ritual takes place and a circle is cast.)

In a coven, the Goddess is represented by the High
Priestess, and the Horned God by the High Priest.

The Goddess is known by many different names. She
is often called Diana, Cerridwen, Freya, Isis, Ishtar, the
Lady, or any other name that a coven chooses to use or
that a Wiccan feels responds to his or her own myth-
opoeic vision.

The Goddess is the female principle. She represents
fertility, creation, the regenerative powers of Nature,
and wisdom. The moon is Her symbol, and in works of
art, She is often depicted as having three faces—each
representing a different lunar phase. In Her new moon
phase, She is the Maiden: in Her full moon phase, She
is the Mother; and in Her waning moon phase, She is
the Crone.

The Horned God is a phallic deity of fertility and
intellectual creativity who symbolizes the powers of the
waxing and waning crescent moons. He is usually represented as a hirsute, bearded man, having the hooves
and horns of a goat. He is a god of Nature, and the male
counterpart to the image of the Goddess. In primitive
times, He was worshipped as the Horned God of Hunting.

Like the Goddess, the Horned God is also known by
many different names. In some Wiccan traditions, He is
called Cernunnos, which is Latin for "the Horned
One." In others, He is known as Pan, Woden, and
other names.

The worship of the Goddess and the Horned God
symbolize the Wiccan belief that everything that exists

in the universe is divided into opposites: female and male, negative and positive, light and darkness, life and death, yin and yang—the balance of Nature.

In certain Wiccan traditions, the Goddess is worshipped during the Spring and Summer Sabbats as She symbolizes the fertility of the earth in the growing time, and the Horned God during the Autumn and Winter Sabbats as He symbolizes the dark half of the year.

Other Wiccan traditions worship the Goddess in Her various aspects throughout the entire year and observe the birth (actually the rebirth) of the Horned God at the Winter Solstice Sabbat; His growth, puberty, and maturity throughout the Spring, Summer, and Autumn Sabbats respectively; and His demise at the Samhain Sabbat. After His death, it is said that His spirit returns to the divine womb of the Mother Goddess until the following Winter Solstice when He is once again reborn. This ancient myth cycle of birth-to-death-to-rebirth repeats each year.

The Horned God has been worshipped since ancient times by nearly all cultures; however, the Roman Catholic Church, in an attempt to eradicate the worship of the old Pagan god of hunting and fertility, perverted Him into their symbol of evil and called Him the Devil.

1

Witchcraft: Past and Present

WITCHCRAFT AND THE DEVIL

The spiritual roots of Wicca can be traced back to paleolithic times when Nature deities were worshipped by all people around the world; however, as a result of the influence of Christianity, anti-Witchcraft church propaganda, and the modification of folk tradition, the Pagan priests and priestesses of early times were transformed into the evil sorcerers and sorceresses of the Middle Ages. And as history clearly proves, it is not unusual for the gods and goddesses of one religion to be turned into the devils and demons of the next. This is most definitely the case with the Old Religion and Christianity.

Unfortunately, as a result of deliberate misconceptions popularized by the Christian realm, the news media, horror movies, talk shows, and so forth, many misinformed people who are not familiar with the actual practices and philosophy of Wicca believe that all Witches are evil. (Some do not even believe that Witches exist in this day and age.) And many people who have either been a victim of ignorance and/or religious brainwashing believe that Witches and modern-day Pagans are involved in one way or another with Satanism and perform blood sacrifices to the old gods or to the Christian's Devil. This is absurd and not true at all! Wiccans definitely *do not* advocate human or animal sacrifice, nor the killing of any living being as an offering to any deity, and as far as the connection between witches and Satanism is concerned, the fact is that real Witches do not worship, receive their powers from, sign pacts with, or sell their souls to the Devil. Actually, Witches do not even acknowledge the existence of the Devil as defined by the Christian religion!

The Devil is an anti-Pagan propaganda device invented by the Christian church. He (or, more appropriately, "it") had never existed in written literature prior to the New Testament. The Craft is a *pre*-Christian religion which has been around much longer than the church or its concept of Satan, who was *never* worshipped as a deity of the Old Religion. The Devil is strictly a part of the Christian belief system, not the Nature-loving earth religion of Wicca.

THE BURNING TIMES

After the Christian Church was formed and came into power, the ways of the Pagans were believed to be a threat to the newly-established religious system, and the worship of the gods of the Old Religion was banned. Ancient Pagan festivals were supplanted by the church's new religious holidays, and the old gods of nature and fertility were turned into hideous and evil demons and devils. (The patriarchal church even changed many of the female Pagan goddesses into evil, *male* demons, not only to vitiate the deities of the Old Religion, but also to erase the fact that the female aspect was ever the object of worship.)

In the year 1233, Pope Gregory IX instituted the Roman Catholic tribunal known as the Inquisition in an attempt to suppress heresy. In 1320, the church (at the request of Pope John XXII) officially declared Witchcraft and the Old Religion of the Pagans as a heretical movement and a "hostile threat" to Christianity. Witches had now become heretics and the persecution against all Pagans spread like wildfire throughout Europe. (It is interesting to note that before a person can be considered a heretic, he or she must first be a Christian, and Pagans have *never* been Christians. They have always been *Pagans*.)

Witches (along with countless numbers of "innocent" men, women, and children who were *not* witches) were persecuted, brutally tortured, often sexually molested or raped, and then executed by sadistic, bloodthirsty church authorities who taught that their God was a god of love and compassion.

Witchcraft in England was made an illegal offense in the year 1541, and in 1604 a law decreeing capital punishment for Witches and Pagans was adopted. Forty years later, the thirteen colonies in American also made death the penalty for the "crime" of Witchcraft. By the late seventeenth century, the followers who remained loyal to the Old Religion were in hiding and Witchcraft had turned into a secret underground religion after an estimated one million persons had been put to death in Europe and more than thirty condemned at Salem, Massachusetts, in the name of Christianity.

Although the infamous Salem Witchcraft trials of 1692 are the most memorable and well-documented ones in the history of the United States of America, the first hanging of a Witch in New England actually took place in Connecticut in 1647, forty-five years prior to the Witchcraft hysteria which plagued Salem Village. Other pre-Salem executions occurred in Providence, Rhode Island, in 1662.

The most popular method of Witch extermination in New England was the gallows. In Europe, it was burning. Other methods included pressing to death, drowning, decapitation, and quartering.

For 260 years following the last Witch execution, the followers of the Old Religion kept their Pagan practices hidden behind the shadows of secrecy, and not until the laws against Witchcraft in England were finally repealed in 1951 did Witches and Pagans officially come out of the broom closet.

WITCHES' LIBERATION

The stereotyped Witch—an ugly, evil, broom-riding hag who eats children and turns people into toads by black magick—is an extremely negative image for which many children's fairy tales and Hollywood horror movies are responsible. Many Witches are tired of and angered by these degrading stereotypes and are fighting the defamation of Witches and the Craft by making themselves public, speaking at seminars, writing books (such as the one you are now reading), and protesting motion pictures, television shows, books, and other things which portray Witches in a negative way and reinforce the stereotyped images. Many Wiccans are legally battling for their constitutional rights and are taking numerous cases of religious discrimination and slander to the courts.

The Witches' liberation movement (which consists of women and men of many ethnic heritages and from all walks of life) has made a great deal of progress in the last ten years. Many colleges and correspondence schools now offer courses in Wicca and occult philosophy. Wiccan support groups, networks, antidiscrimination leagues, and newsletters have sprung up all across the country. Wiccan churches and covens are being recognized in many states as legitimate religious groups entitled to tax-exempt status. The Armed Forces now recognize Wicca as a valid religion, and many Christians (including priests) have publicly defended Wicca as a "positive Earth religion."

Witchcraft (which was officially named "the Old Religion" after the advent of Christianity) has come a long way since its early days; however, the long, hard struggle for religious freedom and social acceptance is far from over. Many Wiccans continue to be discriminated against at their places of employment and in their communities because of their non-Christian religious beliefs. Some children of Wiccan parents are forced to keep their religion a secret or else run the risk of harassment or even expulsion from school. There are isolated cases of physical violence against Wiccans, and in many parts of the world (including certain parts of the United States, surprisingly) it is still against the law for an individual to practice magick, divination, or fortune-telling. For instance, in New York and a few other states any kind of fortune-telling for profit is illegal, and since 1915 the state of Connecticut has had a ridiculous anti-occult law which makes illegal any type of occult activity, whether or not it involves money. In a few states it is actually illegal for one to even admit to having psychic powers (which all human beings have, whether they are developed or not).

In many prison systems throughout the United States

there has even been an ongoing problem for inmates who practice the old ways. The United States Constitution supposedly protects an individual's right to his or her own religious beliefs and practices, yet there are many staff members at various correctional facilities who censor mail with anything pertaining to Wicca, such as Pagan newsletters, books, and Craft lessons from Wiccan correspondence schools. There have even been instances where Pagan prison inmates were refused the right to receive or wear Wiccan religious jewelry.

THE NEW AGE OF WICCA

The time has come for all Wiccans of the world to unite! Be proud! Be happy! Be strong! Be content that you have the courage to follow a path unlike any other in the world. Be comforted in the knowledge that you are not alone. And most important of all, do not be afraid to stand up and fight for your Constitutional rights and religious beliefs. You are a human being who has a legal right to worship the Goddess and the God as you choose.

> Blessed be the children
> of the new age coming
> for all that is created
> by the hands of the Goddess
> shall be theirs
> for all eternity.

> — from *Circle of Shadows*
> By Gerina Dunwich (1990)

2

Sabbat Celebrations

The eight Sabbats celebrated each year by Witches' covens and Solitary Witches are beautiful religious ceremonies which derive from ancient festivals celebrating the change of the seasons.

The Sabbats, also known as the "Great Solar Wheel of the Year" and the "Mandala of Nature," have been celebrated in different forms by nearly all cultures around the world. They are known by various names and are abundant in mythology.

The four major (or grand) Sabbats correspond to the ancient Gaelic year, and are known as: Candlemas, Beltane, Lammas, and Samhain. The four lesser Sabbats are: Spring Equinox, Summer Solstice, Autumn Equinox, and Winter Solstice.

Contrary to the image of the Witches' Sabbat that many people have, it is not a time when Witches gather to have orgies, cast evil spells, or concoct all sorts of weird potions. (Magick is seldom, if ever, performed at a Witches' Sabbat.)

The Sabbat has also, unfortunately, been confused with the Satanic "Black Mass" or "Black Sabbath," which is another example of the misconceptions many people have due to centuries of anti-Pagan church propaganda, fear, ignorance, and the overactive imaginations of writers since the Middle Ages.

A Black Mass is not a Witches' Sabbat. It is a Satanic practice which parodies the central ritual of Catholicism and allegedly includes the sacrifices of unbaptized babies, perverted sexual orgies, and the backward recitation of the Lord's Prayer.

Nothing of this sort ever takes place at the Witches' Sabbats. There are no sacrifices (human or animal), no black magick, and no anti-Catholic rituals. The Sabbats are simply a time when Witches celebrate Nature, dance, sing, feast on traditional Pagan foods, and honor the deities of the Old Religion—mainly the Goddess of Fertility and Her consort, the Horned God. In certain Wiccan traditions, the Goddess is worshipped at the Spring and Summer Sabbats, while the Horned God is worshipped at the Fall and Winter Sabbats.

The celebration of each Sabbat is an intense and sublime spiritual experience which allows Wiccans to be in harmonious balance with the forces of Mother Nature.

The dates on which the eight Witches' Sabbats are celebrated are as follows:

CANDLEMAS SABBAT (also known as Imbolc, Oimelc, and Lady Day) is celebrated on February 2.
SPRING EQUINOX SABBAT (also known as the Vernal Equinox Sabbat, Festival of the Trees, Alban Eilir,

Ostara, and Rite of Eostre) is celebrated on the first day of Spring.

BELTANE SABBAT (also known as May Day, Rood Day, Rudemas, and Walpurgisnacht) is celebrated on May Eve and May 1.

SUMMER SOLSTICE SABBAT (also known as Midsummer, Alban Hefin, and Litha) is celebrated on the first day of Summer.

LAMMAS SABBAT (also known as Lughnasadh, August Eve, and the First Festival of Harvest) is celebrated on August 1.

AUTUMN EQUINOX SABBAT (also known as the Fall Sabbat, Alban Elfed, and the Second Festival of Harvest) is celebrated on the first day of Fall.

SAMHAIN SABBAT (also known as Halloween, Hallowmas, All Hallows' Eve, All Saints' Eve, Festival of the Dead, and the Third Festival of Harvest) is celebrated on October 31.

WINTER SOLSTICE SABBAT (also known as Yule, Winter Rite, Midwinter, and Alban Arthan) is celebrated on the first day of Winter.

(PLEASE NOTE: Each year the astronomical dates of the four lesser Sabbats change. To find out the exact date of each festival, consult an up-to-date astrological calendar or any other current calendar of days showing the exact dates of the equinoxes and solstices.)

Candlemas is a Fire Festival which celebrates the coming of Spring. The aspect of the Goddess invoked at this Sabbat is Brigid, the Celtic goddess of fire, wisdom, poetry, and sacred wells. She is also a deity associated with prophecy, divination, and healing.

This Sabbat also represents new beginnings and spiritual growth, and the "sweeping out of the old" is symbolized by the sweeping of the circle with a besom, or Witch's broom. This is traditionally done by the High

Priestess of the Coven, who wears a brilliant crown of thirteen candles on top of her head.

In Europe, the Candlemas Sabbat was celebrated in ancient times as a torchlight procession to purify and fertilize the fields before the seed-planting season, and to honor and give thanks to the various associated deities and spirits.

The Christianized version of the Candlemas processional honors the Virgin Mary, and in Mexico, it corresponds to the Aztec New Year.

The traditional Pagan foods of the Candlemas Sabbat are foods which represent growth, such as seeds (pumpkin, sesame, sunflower, etc.), poppyseed breads and cakes, and herbal teas.

The **Spring Equinox Sabbat** is a fertility rite celebrating the birth of Spring and the reawakening of life from the earth. On this sacred day, Witches light new fires at sunrise, rejoice, ring bells, and decorate hard-boiled eggs—an ancient Pagan custom associated with the Goddess of Fertility.

Eggs, which are obvious symbols of fertility and reproduction, were used in ancient fertility rites. They were painted with various magickal symbols and then cast into fires or buried in the earth as offerings to the Goddess. In certain parts of the world, Spring Equinox eggs were painted yellow or gold (sacred solar colors) and used in rituals to honor the Sun God.

The aspects of the Goddess invoked at this Sabbat are Eostre (the Saxon goddess of fertility) and Ostara (the German goddess of fertility). In some Wiccan traditions, the fertility deities worshipped on this day are the Green Goddess and the Lord of the Greenwood.

Like most of the old Pagan festivals, Spring Equinox was Christianized by the church into the religious holiday of Easter, which celebrates the resurrection of Jesus Christ.

Easter (which is named after the Saxon fertility deity Eostre) was not officially given the name of the Goddess until the end of the Middle Ages.

To this day, Easter Sunday is determined by the ancient lunar calendar system which places the holiday on the first Sunday after the first full moon on or following the Vernal Spring Equinox. (Formally, this marked the "pregnant" phase of the Triple Goddess passing into the fertile season.)

Easter, like nearly every Christian religious holiday, is rich with an abundance of Pagan overtones, customs, and traditions such as Easter eggs and the Easter bunny. Eggs, as previously mentioned, were ancient fertility symbols and offerings to the goddess of the Pagans. The hare was a symbol of rebirth and resurrection, and was a sacred animal to many lunar goddesses in both western and eastern cultures, including the goddess Ostara, whose escort was a rabbit.

The traditional Pagan foods of the Spring Equinox Sabbat are hard-boiled eggs, honey cakes, the first fruits of the season, and milk punch. In Sweden, waffles are the traditional springtime food.

The **Sabbat of Beltane** is derived from an ancient Druid Fire Festival celebrating the union of the Goddess and Her consort, the Horned God, and thus is also a fertility festival. (In the Old Religion, the word "fertility" signified the desire to produce more from the farms and fields, and not erotic activity per se.)

Beltane also celebrates the returning sun (or Sun God) and is one of the few Pagan festivals that has survived from pre-Christian times to the modern day in much of its original form. It is based in part on Floralia, an old Roman nature festival dedicated to Flora, the sacred goddess of flowers. In more ancient times, this festival day was dedicated to Pluto, the Roman lord of the

Underworld, and counterpart of the god Hades in Greek mythology. The first day of May was also the day when the ancient Romans burned frankincense and Solomon's seal, and hung wildflower wreaths before their altars in honor of the guardian spirits who watched over and protected their families and homes.

On Beltane day, the sun is in the astrological sign of Taurus the Bull, which marks the "death" of Winter, the "birth" of Spring, and the start of the planting season.

Beltane begins with the traditional lighting of Beltane bonfires at moonrise on May Day eve to light the way for Summer. A Sabbat ritual in honor of the Goddess and Horned God is performed, followed by a celebration of Nature which consists of feasts, old Pagan games, poetry readings, and the singing of sacred songs. Various offerings are made to elemental spirits, and coven members exuberantly dance clockwise around a decorated Maypole (a phallic fertility symbol). They also intertwine bright colored ribbons to symbolize the union of male and female and to celebrate the great fertilizing power of the Horned God. The mirth and merriment continues into the wee morning hours, and at dawn on May Day, morning dew is gathered from grass and wildflowers to be used in mystical potions for good luck.

The traditional Pagan foods of the Beltane Sabbat are red fruits (such as cherries and strawberries), herbal salads, red or pink wine punch, and large, round oatmeal or barley cakes known as Beltane cakes.

In the days of the ancient Druids, the Beltane cakes were divided into equal portions, drawn by lot, and consumed as part of the Sabbat rite. Before the ceremony, a portion of the cake would be blackened with charcoal, and whoever was unlucky enough to draw the "black bit" was called the "Beltane carline" and became the sacrificial victim to be thrown into the blazing Beltane bonfire.

In the Scottish Highlands, Beltane cakes are used in divination, and pieces of the cake are often cast into the Beltane bonfire as an offering to the protective spirits and deities.

Summer Solstice (also known as Saint John's Day in Europe) marks the longest day of the year when the Sun is at its zenith. For Witches and Pagans, this sacred day symbolizes the power of the sun which marks an important turning point on the Great Solar Wheel of the Year, for after the Solstice of Summer, the days grow visibly shorter.

In certain Wiccan traditions, the Summer Solstice symbolizes the end of the reign of the waxing year's Oak-King who is now replaced by his successor, the Holly-King of the waning year. (The Holly-King will rule until the Winter Sabbat of Yule, the shortest day of the year.)

The Summer Solstice is the traditional time when Witches harvest magickal herbs for spells and potions, for it is believed that the innate power of herbs are strongest on this day. It is the ideal time for divinations, healing rituals, and the cutting of divining rods and wands. All forms of magick (especially love-magick) are also extremely potent on Summer Solstice Eve, and it is believed that whatever is dreamt of on this night will come true for the dreamer.

The traditional Pagan foods of the Summer Solstice Sabbat are fresh vegetables, Summer fruits, pumpernickel bread, ale, and mead.

Lammas is the first Festival of Harvest. On this Sabbat (which marks the start of the harvest season and is dedicated to bread), Witches give thanks to the gods for the harvest (often with various offerings to the deities to ensure the continued fertility of the land) and honor the fertility aspect of the sacred union of the Goddess and Her consort, the Horned God.

Lammas was originally celebrated by the ancient Druid priests as the festival of Lughnasadh. On this sacred day, they performed rituals of protection and paid homage to Lugh, the Celtic god of the sun. In other pre-Christian cultures, Lammas was celebrated as a festival of grain, and as a day to honor the death of the Sacred King.

The making of corn dollies (small figures fashioned from braided straw) is an old Pagan custom which is carried on by many modern-day Witches as part of the Lammas Sabbat rite. The corn dollies (or kirn babies, as they are sometimes called) are placed on the Sabbat altar to symbolize the Mother Goddess of the harvest. It is customary on each Lammas to make (or buy) a new corn dolly and then burn the old one from the past year for good luck.

The traditional Pagan foods of the Lammas Sabbat are homemade breads (wheat, oat, and especially corn bread), barley cakes, nuts, wild berries, apples, rice, roasted lamb, berry pies, elderberry wine, ale, and meadowsweet tea.

The **Autumn Equinox Sabbat** is the second Festival of Harvest, and the time to celebrate the completion of the grain harvest which began at Lammas. It is also a time for thanksgiving, meditation, and introspection.

On this sacred day, Witches rededicate themselves to the Craft, and Wiccan initiation ceremonies are performed by the High Priestesses and Priests of covens.

Many Wiccan traditions perform a special rite for the goddess Persephone's descent into the Underworld as part of their Autumn Equinox celebration. According to ancient myth, on the day of the Autumn Equinox, Hades (the Greek god of the Underworld) came upon

Persephone, who was picking flowers. He was so taken by her youthful beauty that he instantly fell in love with her. He snatched her up, raped her, and then carried her off in his chariot to the darkness of his domain to rule eternally by his side as his immortal Queen of the Underworld. The goddess Demeter searched everywhere for her abducted daughter, and when she could not find Persephone, her sorrow was so intense that she caused the flowers and trees to wither and die. The great gods of Olympus negotiated Persephone's return, but while in Hades, she had been tricked into eating a small pomegranite seed and therefore had to spend half of each year with Hades in the Underworld for all eternity.

The traditional Pagan foods of the Autumn Equinox Sabbat are corn and wheat products, breads, nuts, vegetables, apples, roots (carrots, onions, potatoes, etc.), cider, and pomegranites (to bless Persephone's journey into the dark realm of the Underworld).

Samhain (pronounced "sow-en") is the most important of all eight Witches' Sabbats. As Halloween, it is one of the best known of all Sabbats outside the Wiccan community, and the most misunderstood and feared.

Samhain celebrates the end of the Goddess-ruled Summer and marks the arrival of the God-ruled Winter. (The name Samhain means "Summer's End.")

Samhain is also the ancient Celtic/Druid New Year, the beginning of the cider season, and a solemn rite and festival of the dead. It is the time when spirits of deceased loved ones and friends are honored, and at one time in history, many believed that it was the night when the dead returned to walk among the living. Samhain night is the ideal time to make contact with, and receive messages from, the spirit world.

The Christianized version of Samhain is All Saints' Day (November 1), which was introduced by Pope

Boniface IV in the seventh century to supplant the Pagan festival. All Souls' Day (which falls on November 2) is another Christian adaptation on the ancient Festival of the Dead. It is observed by the Roman Catholic Church as a sacred day of prayer for souls in purgatory.

In many parts of England, it was believed that the ghosts of all persons who were destined to die in the coming year could be seen walking through the graveyards at midnight on Samhain. Many of the ghosts were thought to be of an evil nature, and so for protection, jack-o'-lanterns with hideous candle-lit faces were carved out of pumpkins and carried as lanterns to scare away the malevolent spirits. In Scotland, the traditional Hallows jack-o'-lantern was carved out of turnips.

An old Samhain custom in Belgium was to prepare special "Cakes for the Dead" (small white cakes or cookies). A cake was eaten for each spirit honored with the belief that the more cakes you ate, the more the dead would bless you.

Another old Samhain custom was to light a fire on the household hearth which would burn continuously until the first day of the following Spring. Huge bonfires were also lit on the hilltops at sunset in honor of the old gods and goddesses, and to guide the souls of the dead home to their kin.

It was on Samhain that the Druids tallied their livestock and mated their ewes for the coming Spring. Surplus breeding stock were sacrificed to the fertility deities and wicker effigies of people and horses were burned as sacrificial offerings.

It is said that lighting a new orange-colored candle at midnight on Samhain and allowing it to burn until sunrise will bring one good luck; however, according to an old legend, bad luck will befall those who bake bread on this day or journey after sunset.

The divinatory arts of scrying (crystal gazing) and

rune-casting on the magickal night of Samhain are Wiccan traditions, as is standing before a mirror and making a secret wish.

The traditional Pagan foods of the Samhain Sabbat are apples, pumpkin pie, hazelnuts, Cakes for the Dead, corn, cranberry muffins and breads, ale, cider, and herbal teas.

The **Winter Solstice Sabbat** (Yule) is the longest night of the year, marking the time when the days begin to grow longer and the hours of darkness decrease. It is the festival of the sun's rebirth, and a time to honor the Horned God. (The aspect of the God invoked at this Sabbat by certain Wiccan traditions is Frey, the Scandinavian fertility god and a deity associated with peace and prosperity.) Love, family togetherness, and accomplishments of the past year are also celebrated.

On this Sabbat, Witches bid farewell to the Great Mother and welcome the reborn Horned God who rules the "dark half of the year."

In ancient times, the Winter Solstice corresponded with the Roman Saturnalia (December 17–24), Pagan fertility rites, and various rites of sun-worship.

The modern day customs that are associated with the Christian religious holiday of Christmas, such as decorating the tree, hanging mistletoe and holly, and burning the Yule log, are all beautiful Pagan customs which date back to pre-Christian times. (Christmas, which takes place just days after the Winter Solstice and celebrates the spiritual birth of Jesus Christ, is actually the Christianized version of the ancient Pagan Yuletide feast.)

The burning of the Yule log stems from the old custom of the Yule bonfire which was burned to give life and power to the sun, which was thought of as being reborn at the Winter Solstice. In later times, the outdoor bonfire custom was replaced by the indoor burning of logs and red candles etched with carvings of solar designs and other magickal symbols. As the oak tree was considered to be the Cosmic Tree of Life by the ancient Druids, the Yule log is traditionally oak. Some Wiccan traditions use a pine Yule log to symbolize the dying gods Attis, Dionysus, or Woden. In days of old, the ashes of the Yule log were mixed with cow fodder to aid in symbolic reproduction and were sprinkled over the fields to ensure new life and a fertile Spring.

The hanging of mistletoe over doorways is a favorite Christmas tradition rich in Pagan symbolism, and another example of how modern Christianity has adapted many of the ancient customs from the Old Religion of the Pagans.

Mistletoe was considered very magickal by the Druids, who called it the "Golden Bough." They believed it possessed great healing powers and gave mortal men access to the Underworld. The living plant, which is actually a parasitic shrub with leathery evergreen leaves and waxy white berries, was at one time thought of as the genitalia of the great god Zeus, whose sacred tree is the oak. The phallic significance of mistletoe stems from the idea that its white berries were drops of the God's divine semen in contrast to the red berries of the holly, which were equated with the sacred menstrual blood of the Goddess. The life-giving essence which the mistletoe suggests provides a symbolic divine substance and a sense of immortality to those who hang it at Yuletide. In ancient times, ecstatic sexual orgies frequently accompanied the rites of the oak-god; in modern times, however, the custom of kissing under the mistletoe is all that remains.

The relatively modern tradition of decorating the Christmas tree is a custom which evolved from the pine groves associated with the Great Mother Goddess. The lights and ornaments hung on the tree as decorations are actually symbols of the sun, moon, and stars as they appear in the Cosmic Tree of Life. They also represent departed souls who are remembered at the end of the year. Sacred presents (which evolved into modern day Christmas gifts) were also hung on the tree as offerings to various deities such as Attis and Dionysus.

In another example of the Pagan roots of Christian holidays, even the modern personification of the Christmas spirit known as Santa Claus was at one time the Pagan god of Yule. To the Scandinavians, he was once known as "Christ on the Wheel," an ancient Norse title for the Sun God who was reborn at the time of the Winter Solstice.

Placing cakes in the boughs of the oldest apple trees in the orchard and pouring on cider as a libation was an old Pagan Yuletide custom practiced in England, and known as "Wassailing the Orchard Trees." It was said that the cider was a substitute for the human or animal blood offered in primitive times as part of a Winter Solstice fertility rite. After offering a toast to the health of the apple trees and giving thanks to them for producing fruit, the farmers would then enjoin the trees to continue producing abundantly.

The traditional Pagan foods of the Winter Solstice Sabbat are roasted turkey, nuts, fruitcakes, caraway rolls, eggnog, and mulled wine.

SABBAT INCENSE

CANDLEMAS: basil, myrrh, and wisteria.
SPRING EQUINOX: African violet, jasmine, rose, sage, and strawberry.
BELTANE: frankincense, lilac, and rose.
SUMMER SOLSTICE: frankincense, lemon, myrrh, pine, rose, and wisteria.
LAMMAS: aloes, rose, and sandalwood.

AUTUMN EQUINOX: benzoin, myrrh, and sage.
SAMHAIN: apple, heliotrope, mint, nutmeg, and sage.
WINTER SOLSTICE: bayberry, cedar, pine, and rosemary.

SABBAT CANDLE COLORS

CANDLEMAS: brown, pink, red.
SPRING EQUINOX: gold, green, yellow.
BELTANE: dark green.
SUMMER SOLSTICE: blue, green.
LAMMAS: orange, yellow.
AUTUMN EQUINOX: brown, green, orange, yellow.
SAMHAIN: black, orange.
WINTER SOLSTICE: gold, green, red, white.

SACRED SABBAT GEMSTONES

CANDLEMAS: amethyst, garnet, onyx, turquoise.
SPRING EQUINOX: amethyst, aquamarine, bloodstone, red jasper.
BELTANE: emerald, orange carnelian, sapphire, rose quartz.
SUMMER SOLSTICE: all green gemstones, especially emerald and jade.
LAMMAS: aventurine, citrine, peridot, sardonyx.
AUTUMN EQUINOX: carnelian, lapis lazuli, sapphire, yellow agate.
SAMHAIN: all black gemstones, especially jet, obsidian, and onyx.
WINTER SOLSTICE: cat's-eye and ruby.

3

The Tools and Symbols of Wicca Craft

TOOLS

THE ATHAME

The athame (also known as an "air dagger") is a ritual knife with a black handle and a double-edged blade which is traditionally engraved or etched with various magickal and/or astrological symbols.

It represents the ancient and mystical element of air, is symbolic of the Life Force, and is used by Witches to draw circles, to exorcise evil and negative forces, to control and banish elemental spirits, and to store and direct energy during magickal rituals.

An athame with a *white* handle is used only for cutting wands, harvesting herbs for magick or healing, carving the traditional Samhain jack-o'-lantern, and carving runes and other magickal or astrological symbols on candles and talismans.

THE BELL

A consecrated brass or crystal bell is often used by Witches to signal the beginning and/or close of a ritual or Sabbat, to summon a particular spirit or deity, and to awaken meditating coven members. Bells are also rung at many Wiccan funeral rites to bless the soul of the Witch who has crossed over to the realm of the dead.

THE BOOK OF SHADOWS

The Book of Shadows (also known as the "Black Book") is a secret diary in which a Witch records his or her personal spells, invocations, rituals, dreams, recipes for various potions, and so forth.

A Book of Shadows may be kept by an individual Witch or by an entire coven.

In the event of a Witch's death, the Book of Shadows may be passed down to his or her children or grandchildren, kept by the High Priestess and High Priest of the coven (if the Witch was a member of one at the time of his or her death), or burned in order to protect the secrets of the Craft. Whichever course of action is taken, of course, depends entirely upon the customs of the particular Wiccan tradition and/or the Witch's own personal wishes.

THE BURIN

The burin is an engraving tool used by many witches
(and Ceremonial Magicians) to mark sacred names,
numbers, runes, and various magickal and/or astrological symbols ritually on their athames, swords, brass
altar bells, metallic jewelry, and other tools of magick
and ritual

THE CAULDRON

The cauldron is a small, black, cast-iron pot that symbolically combines the influences of the four ancient and
mystical elements, represents the divine womb of the
Mother Goddess, and is used by Witches for various
purposes, including brewing potions, burning incense,
and holding charcoal, flowers, herbs, or other magickal
things.

The cauldron can also be used as a tool of divination.
(Many Witches fill their cauldrons with water on Samhain night and use them as magick-mirrors to gaze into
the future or the past.)

THE CEREMONIAL SWORD

The ceremonial sword represents the element of fire
and is the symbol of the Witch's strength.

In certain Wiccan traditions, the ceremonial sword is
used in place of the black-hilted athame by the High
Priestess of a coven both to cast and uncast the circle.

The ceremonial sword, like the athame, can also be
used to control and banish elemental spirits (especially
in Ceremonial Magick), and to store and direct energy
during magickal rituals.

THE CHALICE

The chalice (also known as the sacred cup or goblet) represents the element of air, and is used on the altar during magickal rituals and Sabbats as a container for consecrated water or wine. The sacred chalice is traditionally made of silver, and decorated with various magickal symbols; however, many modern Witches use chalices made of brass, pewter, or even crystal.

THE PENTACLE

The pentacle is a flat disc made of wood, wax, metal, or clay. It bears the motif of the mystical five-pointed Witch's star (pentagram), and is used in magickal ceremonies and spells to represent feminine energy and the element of earth, to invoke and bind gnomes (elemental spirits of the earth), and also to hold consecrated objects such as amulets, herbs, crystals, and so forth.

THE WAND

The magick wand (also known as a "firestick") is a slender wooden rod fashioned from the branch of a tree. It represents the ancient and mystical element of fire, and is a symbol of the strength, will, and magickal power of the Witch who possesses it. In ceremonial Magick, the wand represents the element of air.

The wand (which, according to many ancient grimoires of magick, should be approximately twenty-one inches in length) is used by Witches to invoke salamanders (the elemental spirits of the fire element) in certain types of rituals, trace circles, draw magickal symbols on the ground, direct energy, and stir cauldron brews.

Fashioning a wand from a branch of the appropriate tree is essential, for different types of wood possess different magickal properties. Ash wands are appropriate for use in healing rituals and all forms of white magick. Elder wands are appropriate for use in consecrations and exorcisms. Acacia wands and hazel wands are appropriate for use in all forms of white magick. Oak wands (sacred to the ancient Druid priests) are appropriate for use in all forms of Druidic and solar magick. Willow wands and rowan wands (both sacred to all Lunar Goddesses) are appropriate for use in lunar magick, Goddess invocations, wish-magick, and psychic healing rituals.

OTHER IMPORTANT TOOLS

Other important tools of Wicca craft are candles (symbolic of the element fire); a thurible or censer of incense (symbolic of the element air, and ritually burned as an offering to the Goddess and the Horned God, to invoke Sylphs, which are the elemental spirits of air, and to create the proper mystical atmosphere for spellcasting or invoking); a dish of salt (symbolic of the earth element, and used for purification); and a black or white hooded robe to wear during rituals and Sabbats (unless, of course, you prefer to work skyclad or nude.)

SYMBOLS

Symbols are an important part of both the religious and magickal aspects of Wicca. They are marked on robes, candles, ritual tools, amulets, and talismans, and are ritually used by Witches to alter their consciousness and to produce magickal energy.

The signs of the zodiac and of the planets are often used in Wicca, as are the following symbols:

The *Crescent Moon* is a sacred symbol of the Goddess, and also a symbol of magick, feminine energy, fertility, abundant growth, and the secret powers of Nature. It is used in invocations of the Goddess and all lunar deities (both male and female), moon-magick, Sabbat celebrations, and women's healing rituals.

The *Pentagram* is one of the most powerful and popular Pagan symbols used by Witches and Ceremonial Magicians alike. The pentagram (a five-pointed star within a circle) represents the four mystical and ancient elements of fire, water, air, and earth, surmounted by the Spirit.

In Wicca, the pentagram symbol is *usually* drawn with its point facing upwards to symbolize human spiritual aspirations. A pentagram with its point facing down is a symbol of the Horned God.

The *Triangle* is a symbol of finite manifestation in Western magick and is used in rituals to evoke spirits when the seal or sign of the entity to be summoned is placed in the center of the triangle.

The triangle, equivalent to the number three (a powerful magickal number), is also a sacred symbol of the Triple Goddess: Maiden, Mother, Crone. Inverted, it represents the male principle.

The *Seal of Solomon* (an ancient and powerful magickal symbol) is a hexagram consisting of two interlocking triangles, one facing up and the other facing down. It symbolizes the human soul, and is used by many Witches and Ceremonial Magicians in spells and rituals involving spirit communications, wisdom, purification, and the strengthening of psychic powers.

The *Trident* is a sacred triple-phallus symbol which is displayed by any male deity whose function is to sexually unite with the Triple Goddess. It is used primarily in Great Rites, sex-magick, and fertility rituals.

The *Ankh* is an ancient Egyptian symbol resembling a cross with a loop at the top. It symbolizes life, cosmic knowledge, sexual intercourse, and rebirth. (Every major god and goddess of the ancient Egyptian pantheon is depicted carrying it.) Also known as the "Crux Ansata," it is used by many contemporary Witches in spells and rituals involving health, fertility, and divination.

The *Eye of Horus* is another ancient Egyptian symbol which is often used in contemporary Witchcraft. It depicts the divine eye of the god Horus, represents both solar and lunar energies, and is often used to symbolize spiritual protection as well as the clairvoyant power of the Third Eye.

The *Pentalpha* is a magickal design formed by interlocking five A's. It is used by many Witches and Ceremonial Magicians in both divination and the conjuration of spirits.

The *Circle* (a highly potent image possessing neither beginning nor end) is used by many Witches and neo-Pagans as a sacred symbol of the yoni, magickal energy, protection, infinity, perfection, and constant renewal.

The *Swastika* is an ancient religious symbol formed by a Greek cross with the arms bent at right angles in either a clockwise or counterclockwise direction. Before being adopted and perverted in 1935 as the infamous official emblem of Nazi Germany, the Swastika was a sacred symbol of good luck and health in pre-Christian Europe and in many other Pagan cultures around the world, including the Orientals, the Egyptians, and the Native tribes of North, Central, and South America.

The word "swastika" stems from the Sanskrit *svastika* meaning "a sign of good luck." There are over 1,200 known swastika designs, and the oldest one dates back to the year 12,000 B.C.

In addition to the above-mentioned symbols of magick, there are hundreds of both ancient and modern symbols used in Wicca, such as male and female fertility symbols, crosses, peace signs, numbers, flowers, animals, mythological creatures (dragons, phoenix, unicorn, etc.), the World Tree, and so forth.

SOME OF THE SYMBOLS OF WICCA CRAFT

Swastika

Ankh

Eye of Horus

Seal of Solomon

Triangle

Pentagram

4

Pagan Rituals

RITE OF SELF-DEDICATION
(for Solitary Witches)

(PLEASE NOTE: Before self-initiation into the Craft, it is imperative that a person first study the basic philosophy of Wicca and sincerely feel within his or her heart that the Old Religion is the correct path for him or her to follow.)

If you desire to become a Witch, and are unable to be initiated by a coven (or if you choose to work alone as a Solitary), you may initiate yourself into the Craft and dedicate yourself to the Goddess and Her consort by performing the following Self-Initiation Ritual on a night of the full or waxing moon, on any of the eight Witches' Sabbats, or on your birthday.

Begin by removing your clothes and bathing yourself in a perfumed or herbal ritual bath (symbolic of the element water) to purify your body and spirit of any negative vibrations. As you bathe, clear your mind completely of all mundane, negative and unpleasant thoughts, and meditate until your body is totally relaxed.

After bathing, cast on the floor a circle of about six feet in diameter, using white chalk or paint. Sprinkle a bit of salt (symbolic of the element earth) over the circle to consecrate it, and say:

WITH SALT I CONSECRATE
AND BLESS THIS CIRCLE
IN THE DIVINE NAMES OF THE GODDESS
AND HER CONSORT, THE HORNED GOD.
BLESSED BE!

Sit in the center of the circle, facing north, with two white candles (symbolic of the element fire) and a censer of frankincense and myrrh incense (symbolic of the element air) before you. (It is best to perform this ritual alone and skyclad, or nude; however, if you feel uncomfortable working without clothing on, you may wear a white ceremonial robe instead.)

Light the incense, and then light the first candle, and say:

I INVOKE AND CALL UPON THEE
O MOTHER GODDESS, CREATRESS OF LIFE
AND SOUL OF THE INFINITE UNIVERSE.
BY CANDLE FLAME AND INCENSE SMOKE
DO I INVOKE THEE TO BLESS THIS RITE

AND TO GRANT ME ADMITTANCE
TO THE COMPANY OF THY LOVING CHILDREN

O BEAUTIFUL GODDESS OF LIFE AND REBIRTH
WHO IS KNOWN AS CERRIDWEN, ASTARTE,
  ATHENE,
BRIGIT, DIANA, ISIS, MELUSINE, APHRODITE,
AND BY MANY OTHER DIVINE NAMES,
IN THIS CONSECRATED CIRCLE OF CANDLELIGHT
I DO PLEDGE MYSELF TO HONOR THEE,
TO LOVE THEE, AND TO SERVE THEE WELL
FOR AS LONG AS I SHALL LIVE
I PROMISE TO RESPECT AND OBEY THY LAW
OF LOVE UNTO ALL LIVING THINGS.
I PROMISE NEVER TO REVEAL CRAFT SECRETS
TO ANY MAN OR WOMAN NOT OF THE SAME
  PATH;
AND I SWEAR TO ABIDE BY THE WICCAN REDE;
"AN IT HARM NONE, DO WHAT THOU WILT."

O GODDESS, QUEEN OF ALL WITCHES,
I DO OPEN MY HEART AND SOUL TO THEE.
SO MOTE IT BE.

Light the second candle, and say:

I INVOKE AND CALL UPON THEE
O GREAT HORNED GOD OF PAGANS,
LORD OF THE GREEN WOODLANDS
AND FATHER OF ALL THINGS WILD AND FREE.
BY CANDLE FLAME AND INCENSE SMOKE
DO I INVOKE THEE TO BLESS THIS RITE.
O GREAT HORNED GOD OF DEATH
AND ALL THAT COMES AFTER
WHO IS KNOWN AS CERNUNNOS, ATTIS, PAN,
DAGHDA, FAUNUS, FREY, ODIN, LUPERCUS,

AND BY MANY OTHER NAMES,
IN THIS CONSECRATED CIRCLE OF CANDLELIGHT
I DO PLEDGE MYSELF TO HONOR THEE,
TO LOVE THEE, AND TO SERVE THEE WELL
FOR AS LONG AS I SHALL LIVE.

O GREAT HORNED GOD OF PEACE AND LOVE
I DO OPEN MY HEART AND SOUL TO THEE.
SO MOTE IT BE.

Hold your open hands up to the heavens. Close your eyes and visualize two white beams of glowing light streaking down from the sky and flowing into your palms. A warm, tingling feeling will begin to spread throughout your body as the love power of the Goddess and the God purifies your soul.

Do not be afraid if you begin to hear a voice (or voices) speaking inside your mind as if by telepathy. It is the Goddess and the God within you making their presence known. (Although not every Wiccan hears or perceives the actual spoken words of the Goddess and the Horned God—some merely feel their divine presence and love—it is not uncommon for the Pagan deities to speak directly to a newly self-initiated Witch, especially if he or she is psychic-sensitive to begin with.)

Remain in the consecrated circle until both of the candles and the incense have burned themselves out.

The Wiccan Rite of Self-Initiation is now ended.

CRYSTAL CONSECRATION RITUAL

Perform the following ritual on a night of the full moon to cleanse a crystal of negative influences and to charge it with healing power.

Begin by lighting two white altar candles (one on each

side of the altar). Place a small bowl or cup of fresh rainwater (or melted snow) and a dish of sand, soil, or salt on the altar. In the center of the altar, place a censer containing any of the following incenses: frankincense, myrrh, nutmeg, patchouli, rose, saffron, or sandalwood.

Take the crystal in your right hand and pass it through the smoke of the incense as you say:

> BY THE POWER OF THE GODDESS
> AND BY THE ANCIENT AND MYSTICAL
>   ELEMENT OF AIR
> I CONSECRATE AND DEDICATE
> THIS CRYSTAL AS A MAGICKAL TOOL
>   OF HEALING.

Gently place the crystal in the dish of sand, soil, or salt, and say:

> BY THE POWER OF THE HORNED GOD
> AND BY THE ANCIENT AND MYSTICAL
>   ELEMENT OF EARTH
> I CONSECRATE AND DEDICATE
> THIS CRYSTAL AS A MAGICKAL TOOL OF
>   HEALING

Sprinkle a few drops of water on the crystal, and say:

> BY THE POWER OF THE UNIVERSE
> AND BY THE ANCIENT AND MYSTICAL
>   ELEMENT OF WATER
> I CONSECRATE AND DEDICATE
> THIS CRYSTAL AS A MAGICKAL TOOL
>   OF HEALING.

Once again, take the crystal in your right hand. Move it in a sunwise circle around the flame of each candle as you say:

BY THE POWER OF LOVE
AND BY THE ANCIENT AND MYSTICAL
  ELEMENT OF FIRE
I CONSECRATE AND DEDICATE
THIS CRYSTAL AS A MAGICKAL TOOL
  OF HEALING.

MAY THIS CRYSTAL STONE OF POWER
WORK FOR MY GOOD
AND FOR THE GOOD OF ALL.
SO MOTE IT BE.

After the consecration ritual has been performed, cup the crystal between your hands and allow it to harmonize with your aura and spiritual consciousness. Breathe gently upon the crystal as you direct your thoughts and intentions into it. The charged crystal will respond to the energy of your will.

INVOCATION AND RITE OF HECATE

Hecate, the mysterious Goddess of Darkness and protectress of all Witches, is a personification of the moon and the dark side of the female principle. Her name is Greek, meaning "she who succeeds from afar," which links her with Diana (Artemis), the virgin huntress of the moon.

In mythology, Hecate was the daughter of the Titans Perses and Asteria, and She was believed to roam the earth and haunt crossroads on moonless nights with a pack of ghostly, howling dogs.

Like Diana, Hecate belongs to the class of torch-bearing deities, and was conceived as carrying a burning torch to suit the belief that she was the nocturnal lunar goddess and a mighty huntress who knew her way in the realm of spirits. She controlled the phases of birth, life and death, and it is said that the secret powers of Nature were at her command.

Although dogs were the animals most sacred to her, Hecate was associated with hares in ancient Greece, as was her German equivalent, the lunar-goddess Harek. (The hare, according to a series of Egyptian hieroglyphs, is a "determinative sign defining the concept of being, and symbolic in consequence of elemental existence." To the ancient Chinese, the hare was believed to be an animal of augury and it was said to live on the moon.)

In art, Hecate is often depicted as a three-headed woman with hissing serpents entwined about her neck. For this reason she is called a Triformis—a symbol which may be related to the three levels of Birth, Life, and Death (representing the Past, the Present, and the Future) and to the Triple Goddess trinity of Maiden, Mother, and Crone.

Hecate is a powerful lunar deity, and all rituals performed in her honor should be held at midnight on moonless nights or at moonrise on August 13, the major Pagan festival of Hecate.

Before beginning the following invocation and ritual, find a secluded spot in the clearing of a dark, quiet, wooded area and cast a circle of stones about nine to thirteen feet in diameter. At the north point of the circle, erect a small altar. Place a Goddess symbol (such as a small female statuette or figurine) on top of the altar and light frankincense, myrrh or jasmine incense before it. To the left of the Goddess symbol, place a black altar candle and a chalice of white wine. To the right of the

Goddess symbol, place another black altar candle, a consecrated athame, a brass altar bell, a bowl of water and a dish containing sea salt. White elemental candles should be placed at each of the east, south and west points of the circumference of the circle. An elemental candle representing the north should be placed behind the Goddess figure on the altar.

The High Priestess (or Solitary) lights the candles and then blesses the water by dipping the blade of the athame into the bowl of water and saying:

I EXORCISE THEE
O CREATURE OF WATER
IN THE DIVINE NAME OF HECATE
AND I CAST OUT FROM THEE
ALL IMPURITIES AND UNCLEAN SPIRITS.
SO MOTE IT BE.

The High Priestess puts the tip of the athame into the salt and purifies it by saying:

BLESSED BE THIS SALT
IN THE NAME OF GODDESS HECATE.
LET ALL MALIGNITY AND HINDRANCE
BE CAST FORTH HENCEFROM
AND LET ALL GOOD ENTER HEREIN.
SO MOTE IT BE.

The athame is returned to the altar and the salt is then poured into the bowl of water.

The High Priestess traces the circle with her sword in a clockwise direction, saying:

I CONJURE THEE, O CIRCLE OF POWER
THAT THOU BEIST A RING OF PROTECTION
THAT SHALL PRESERVE AND CONTAIN

THE POWER THAT WE SHALL RAISE WITHIN THEE;
A SHIELD AGAINST ALL WICKEDNESS AND EVIL
WHEREFORE I DO BLESS THEE
AND CONSECRATE THEE IN THE NAME OF
  HECATE:
GODDESS OF DARKNESS
GODDESS OF THE MOON.

The High Priest lights a fire in the center of the circle
and places upon it a cauldron painted with moon symbols and filled with a fragrant mixture of well water,
rose oil, and honey. The brew is brought to a boil and
then the High Priestess drops in a pinch of powdered
moonstone, the feathers of a black crow, hoarfrost gathered by moonlight, and the mystical moon-ruled plants
of nightshade and moonwart. (The original cauldron
ingredients in the ancient version of the Hecate ritual
called for the entrails of a wolf in addition to the things
just mentioned; however, this particular ingredient has
been omitted from the modern version as it would be
extremely difficult as well as dangerous for the average
Witch to obtain.)

After all of the ingredients have been put in, the
bubbling brew is stirred with a dry olive branch. The
High Priestess stands before the cauldron facing North
with her arms outstretched and says:

  I DO BID THEE
  O UNSEEN FORCES OF NATURE
  TO GATHER ROUND ME IN THIS CIRCLE
  FOR IN THIS MYSTICAL HOUR OF NIGHT
  I DO CALL FORTH THE DARK GODDESS
  OF THE MOON.

  I INVOKE AND CONJURE THEE, HECATE

QUEEN OF THE UNDERWORLD
AND PROTECTRESS OF ALL WITCHES.
COME NOW INTO THIS CIRCLE OF FIRE
AS I DO PERFORM THIS RITE
IN YOUR HONOR.

The entire coven kneels before the altar, facing the image of the Goddess as the High Priestess takes up the chalice of wine in both hands and says:

IN HONOR OF THEE
O GREAT GODDESS HECATE
DO I POUR THIS LIBATION
AND DRINKETH THIS TOAST.

The High Priestess pours a few drops of the wine onto the ground in front of the altar as an offering to the Goddess. She raises the chalice to her lips, drinks a bit of the wine, and then hands the chalice to the High Priest who sips the wine and then returns the chalice to its place on the altar. He takes the bell and rings it thrice as the High Priestess takes the athame in her right hand, points it up to the sky and says:

IN THIS DARK AND MYSTICAL HOUR OF NIGHT
DOES THE GODDESS HECATE REIGN SUPREME
AND IN HER NAME DO I NOW GIVE PRAISE:
HAIL TO THEE, HECATE!
HAIL TO THEE, HECATE!
BLESSED BE!

The High Priestess kisses the blade of the athame and then returns it to the altar as the coven repeats the chant:

                HAIL TO THEE, HECATE!
                HAIL TO THEE, HECATE!
BLESSED BE!

The entire coven should now relax and meditate upon the image of the Goddess. Pagan folk songs may now be sung in her honor or mystical Goddess-inspired poetry recited.

After the rite has concluded, the coven gives thanks to the Goddess for her presence and then the High Priestess uncasts the circle with the sword moving in a counterclockwise direction.

THIRD EYE RITUAL

Perform this neo-Pagan ritual to improve psychic powers three days before the moon is full, and preferably when it is in either the astrological sign of Cancer, Pisces, or Scorpio.

Begin by brewing a strong magickal tea made from yarrow or mugwort (herbs which stimulate the psychic senses) and then light thirteen purple-colored votive candles to help attract psychic influences.

Drink the tea and then gaze fixedly into a magick mirror, crystal ball, or crystal pyramid as you chant thrice the following incantation:

    I INVOKE THEE, O ASARIEL
    ARCHANGEL OF NEPTUNE
    AND RULER OF CLAIRVOYANT POWERS.
    I ASK THEE NOW TO OPEN MY THIRD EYE
    AND SHOW ME THE HIDDEN LIGHT.
    LET ME SEE THE FUTURE.
    LET ME SEE THE PAST.
    LET ME PERCEIVE THE DIVINE

KINGDOMS OF THE UNKNOWN.
LET ME UNDERSTAND THE WISDOM
OF THE MIGHTY UNIVERSE.
SO MOTE IT BE.

After chanting, relax, breathe slowly and concentrate on opening your Third Eye. Do not permit any negative thoughts to contaminate your mind.

The Third Eye, an invisible chakra located in the middle of the forehead above the space between the eyebrows, is the human body's highest source of power, supernormal sight, and clairvoyant vision.

THE GREAT RITE

The Great Rite (also known as the "sacred marriage") is ritual sexual intercourse which is performed either actually or symbolically as a sublime religious experience.

This major male/female "polarity" ritual is often enacted at major Sabbats (especially Samhain by the High Priestess and the High Priest who draw down into themselves the spirit of the Goddess and the Horned God, respectively, and experience a divine union that is both spiritual and physical.

In certain Wiccan traditions (such as the Gardnerians), the Great Rite is performed as part of the Third Degree Initiation, which promotes a Witch to the highest of the three grades of the Craft.

The Actual Great Rite: After a Goddess invocation has been delivered by the High Priest, the coven members leave the circle and the room, and the High Priestess and High Priest privately engage in ritual lovemaking. After the Great Rite has been performed, the coveners are readmitted to the circle, and consecrated cakes and wine (or ale) are served.

The Symbolic Great Rite: After a Goddess invocation
has been delivered by the High Priest, he dips the blade
of his athame into a goblet of wine (or fruit juice) which
is held by the High Priestess. The wine is then passed
around and drunk by all members of the coven.

DRAWING DOWN THE MOON

Drawing Down the Moon (also known as "Calling
Down the Moon") is the ritual invocation of the God-
dess spirit-force into the High Priestess by the High
Priest who uses his male polarity to conjure forth the
divine essence in the female polarity of the High
Priestess.

During this modern Wiccan ritual, the High Priestess
enters a trance-like altered state of consciousness, and
draws the power of the Goddess into herself. The High
Priestess then functions as a channel of the Goddess or
as the Goddess incarnate within the circle until it has
been uncast.

DRAWING DOWN THE SUN

Drawing Down the Sun (also known as "Calling Down
the Sun" or "Drawing Down the Horned God") is the
ritual invocation of the Horned God spirit-force into the
High Priest by the High Priestess who uses her female
polarity to conjure forth the divine essence in the male
polarity of the High Priest.

During this modern Wiccan ritual, the High Priest
enters a trance-like altered state of consciousness, and
draws the power of the Horned God into himself. The
High Priest then functions as a channel of the Horned
God or as the Horned God incarnate within the circle
until it has been uncast.

PAGAN HANDFASTING RITUAL

Handfasting (sometimes known as handfesting) is an old Wiccan betrothal ceremony in which the hands of the bride and groom are tied together with a consecrated knotted cord to signify that they have been joined together in matrimonial union. The rite is usually performed by either the High Priestess or the High Priest of the coven (if the wedding is nonlegal) or by a legally recognized minister if a legally-binding wedding is preferred. (Before being legally wed, many Wiccan couples prefer to live in a common-law "trial" marriage which can be dissolved by the High Priestess at the end of the year if either the husband or the wife is dissatisfied with the arrangement.)

The Pagan tradition of "Jumping the Broom," in which the bride and groom both jump over a broomstick, is an ancient form of a common-law marriage ceremony practiced in certain parts of Scotland, Denmark, and China, and quite popular among the Gypsies. The Broom Jump is performed at the end of the Handfasting Rite.

The following wedding ceremony is a nonlegally binding spiritual commitment rite which can be performed by either the coven's High Priestess or High Priest.

Before the ceremony is carried out, it is extremely important that the entire area where the handfasting is to take place be consecrated by salt, water, and any purifying incense such as cedar, frankincense, sage, or sandalwood.

Erect the altar and place upon it everything needed for the ceremony: two white candles, a censer of incense, a dish of salt or soil, a brass altar bell, a wand, a chalice of water, a cup of rose oil for anointing, a quartz crystal, the wedding rings, and two white cords. Next to the altar, place a large straw broom to be used in the traditional Broom Jump at the end of the rite.

Cast a circle in a clockwise direction using an athame or ceremonial sword, and after each guest has been blessed with greetings and incense, ring the altar bell to signal the start of the ceremony.

The bride and groom should enter the circle, holding hands. Bless them with incense and greetings, and then have them stand facing you and the altar (north) as the wedding guests gather around the perimeter of the circle, joining all hands together to form a human chain. Facing the bride and groom, raise your arms up to the sky and say:

IN THIS SACRED CIRCLE OF LIGHT
WE GATHER IN PERFECT LOVE
AND PERFECT TRUST.
O GODDESS OF DIVINE LOVE
I ASK THEE TO BLESS THIS COUPLE,
THEIR LOVE, AND THEIR MARRIAGE
FOR AS LONG AS THEY SHALL LIVE
IN LOVE TOGETHER.
MAY THEY EACH ENJOY A HEALTHY LIFE
FILLED WITH JOY, LOVE, STABILITY
AND FERTILITY.

Hold the dish of salt or soil before them and let each of them place their right hand over the dish as you say:

BLESSED BE
BY THE ANCIENT AND MYSTICAL
ELEMENT OF EARTH.
MAY THE GODDESS OF LOVE
IN ALL OF HER GLORY

BLESS YOU WITH LOVE, TENDERNESS,
HAPPINESS AND COMPASSION
FOR AS LONG AS YE BOTH SHALL LIVE.

Return the dish of salt or soil to the altar. The couple now should turn and face east. Ring the altar bell thrice and then smudge the couple with incense, and say:

BLESSED BE BY SMOKE AND BELL,
SYMBOLS OF THE ANCIENT AND MYSTICAL
ELEMENT OF AIR.
MAY THE GODDESS OF LOVE
IN ALL OF HER GLORY
BLESS YOU WITH COMMUNICATION,
INTELLECTUAL GROWTH, AND WISDOM
FOR AS LONG AS YE BOTH SHALL LIVE.

Return the censer of incense to the altar. The couple now should turn and face south. Hand each of them a white candle to hold in their right hand. Light the candles, and then take the wand from the altar and hold it above them as you say:

BLESSED BE BY WAND AND FLAME.
SYMBOLS OF THE ANCIENT AND MYSTICAL
ELEMENT OF FIRE.
MAY THE GODDESS OF LOVE
IN ALL OF HER GLORY
BLESS YOU WITH HARMONY, VITALITY,
CREATIVITY, AND PASSION
FOR AS LONG AS YE BOTH SHALL LIVE.

Return the candles and wand to the altar. The couple now should turn and face west. Take the chalice of

water and sprinkle some of the water over their heads
as you say:

BLESSED BE
BY THE ANCIENT AND MYSTICAL
ELEMENT OF WATER.
MAY THE GODDESS OF LOVE
IN ALL OF HER GLORY
BLESS YOU WITH FRIENDSHIP, INTUITION,
CARING, AND UNDERSTANDING
FOR AS LONG AS YE BOTH SHALL LIVE.

Return the chalice of water to the altar. The couple
once again should turn and face north. Anoint their
foreheads with rose oil, and then hold the quartz crystal
over them as a sacred symbol of the spiritual realm as
you say:

MAY THE DIVINE GODDESS OF LOVE
IN ALL OF HER GLORY
BLESS YE WITH TOGETHERNESS,
HONESTY, AND SPIRITUAL GROWTH
FOR AS LONG AS YE BOTH SHALL LIVE.
MAY THE GOD AND GODDESS WITHIN YE
GUIDE YE ON THE RIGHT PATH
AND MAY THE MAGICK OF YOUR LOVE
CONTINUE TO GROW FOR AS LONG
AS YE REMAIN TOGETHER IN LOVE
FOR YOUR MARRIAGE IS A SACRED UNION
OF THE FEMALE AND MALE ASPECTS
OF DIVINITY.

Return the crystal to the altar and consecrate the
wedding rings with a sprinkle of salt and water as you
say:

BY SALT AND WATER
I PURIFY AND CLEANSE
THESE BEAUTIFUL SYMBOLS OF LOVE.
LET ALL NEGATIVE VIBRATIONS,
IMPURITIES, AND HINDRANCES
BE CAST FORTH HENCEFROM!
AND LET ALL THAT IS POSITIVE,
LOVING, AND GOOD
ENTER HEREIN.
BLESSED BE THESE RINGS
IN THE DIVINE NAME OF THE GODDESS.
SO MOTE IT BE.

The groom now places the bride's ring upon her finger, and she in turn places the other ring on his. They may now exchange their vows, which each has written in his and her own words prior to the ceremony.

After the couple's vows of love have been spoken, consecrate the cords in the same manner as the wedding rings, and then, holding the cords side by side, have the man and woman each take an end and tie a knot as they express their love to each other. Tie it in the middle of the cord and say:

BY THE KNOTS ON THIS CORD
YOUR LOVE IS UNITED.

Take the knotted cord and tie together the hands of the bride and her groom. Visualize a white light of Goddess energy and protection surrounding the couple as their auras join together as one and everyone attending the ceremony raises energy by repeatedly and joyously chanting: LOVE! LOVE! LOVE!

After you have grounded the power raised into the

bride and groom and their marriage, allow for a few
moments of silence, and then remove the cord from
their hands and say:

BY THE POWER OF THE GODDESS
AND HER HORNED CONSORT
I NOW PRONOUNCE YE
HUSBAND AND WIFE
FOR AS LONG AS YE BOTH
SHALL LIVE TOGETHER IN LOVE.
SO MOTE IT BE.

The guests may now cheer, applaud, and congratu-
late the newlywed couple. Give thanks to the Goddess
and God, and then uncast the circle. Lay the straw
broom horizontally on the ground and have the bride
and groom leap over it together as they hold each other's hands.

The Wiccan Handfasting Rite is now ended, and
should be celebrated by all with consecrated wine and a
handfasting cake which is traditionally cut by the cov-
en's ceremonial sword. (See page 147 for Handfasting
Cake recipe.)

CANDLEMAS SABBAT
February 2

Begin by erecting an altar, facing north. Place before it a
consecrated besom (a straw broom). Prepare a crown of
thirteen red candles and place it on the center of the
altar. At each side of the crown, place a candle of the
appropriate Sabbat color. To the left, place a censer of
the appropriate incense and a sprig of evergreen. (A
sprig of the previous year's Yule tree or wreath may also
be used as an altar decoration.) To the right, place a

chalice of water (fresh rainwater or melted snow, if at all possible), a small dish of dirt or sand, and a consecrated athame.

Cast a circle about nine feet in diameter around the altar, using white chalk or paint. Sprinkle a bit of salt inside the circle and then trace the circle in a clockwise direction with a consecrated ceremonial sword, or a willow wand, and say:

WITH SALT AND SACRED SWORD
I CONSECRATE AND INVOKE THEE
O SABBAT CIRCLE OF MAGICK AND LIGHT.
IN THE SACRED NAME OF BRIGIT
AND UNDER HER PROTECTION
IS THIS SABBAT RITE NOW BEGUN.

Place the ceremonial sword on the altar before the crown of candles. Light the two altar candles and say:

O FIRE GODDESS OF SPRING
I OFFER TO THEE
THIS SYMBOL OF FIRE
SO MOTE IT BE.

Light the incense and say:

O FIRE GODDESS OF SPRING
I OFFER TO THEE
THIS SYMBOL OF AIR
SO MOTE IT BE.

Take the athame in your right hand and with the tip of the blade draw a pentacle (five-pointed star) in the dirt or sand, and say:

O FIRE GODDESS OF SPRING
I OFFER TO THEE
THIS SYMBOL OF EARTH
SO MOTE IT BE.

Dip the blade of the athame into the chalice of water and say:

O FIRE GODDESS OF SPRING
I OFFER TO THEE
THIS SYMBOL OF WATER
SO MOTE IT BE.

Return the athame to the altar. Light the sprig of evergreen and visualize in your mind's eye the darkness of Winter burning away, being replaced by the warm light of the new Spring. Place the burning sprig in the censer and say:

AS THIS SYMBOL OF WINTER
IS CONSUMED BY THE FIRE
SO IS THE DARKNESS
CONSUMED BY THE LIGHT.
SO MOTE IT BE.

Light the crown of candles and carefully place it on top of your head. (When this Sabbat ritual is performed by a coven, it is customary for the High Priest to light the candles and place the crown upon the head of the High Priestess.) Take the athame in your right hand and hold it over your heart as you say:

LIKE SWEET CYBELE, I WEAR A CROWN
OF FIRE AROUND MY HEAD.
LIKE DIANA, BLESSED GODDESS WISE

I LIGHT THE CANDLES RED
TO SHINE A LIGHT UPON MY PRAYER
FOR PEACE ON EARTH AND LOVE.
O HEAR ME SPIRITS OF THE AIR.
SPIRITS BELOW AND SPIRITS ABOVE.
SO MOTE IT BE!

Return the athame to the altar and end the rite by sweeping the circle in a counterclockwise direction with the besom to uncast the circle and to symbolize the "sweeping out" of the old. Extinguish the candles and return the crown to the altar.

SPRING EQUINOX SABBAT
First Day of Spring

Begin by casting a circle about nine feet in diameter, using white chalk or paint. Erect an altar in the center of the circle facing north. Place a candle of the appropriate Sabbat color on the middle of the altar. To the right (east) of the candle, place a censer of the appropriate Sabbat incense or a thurible containing a hot charcoal block whereupon sage can be burned. To the left (west) of the candle, place a bowl of hard-boiled eggs decorated with runes, fertility designs, and other magickal symbols. Before the candle (south), place a consecrated athame and a consecrated ceremonial sword.

After sprinkling a bit of salt on the circle to purify it, take the ceremonial sword and trace the circle in a clockwise motion, starting in the east. As you trace the circle, say:

BLESSED BE THIS SABBAT CIRCLE
IN THE DIVINE NAME OF OSTARA
ANCIENT GODDESS OF FERTILITY AND SPRING.

IN HER SACRED NAME
AND UNDER HER PROTECTION
IS THIS SABBAT RITE NOW BEGUN.

Return the sword to the altar, and then light the candle and incense. Take the athame in your right hand and kneel before the altar with the blade of the athame held over your heart, and say:

BLESSED BE THE FERTILITY GODDESS,
BLESSED BE HER SPRINGTIME RITE.
BLESSED BE THE SUN GOD KING,
BLESSED BE HIS SACRED LIGHT.

Place the blade of the athame over the Third Eye region of your forehead, and say:

THE SUN HAS CROSSED THE CELESTIAL EQUATOR,
GIVING SUN AND MOON EQUAL HOURS.
GODDESS SPRING IS REBORN AT LAST,
HER BEAUTY GIVES LIFE
TO THE TREES AND FLOWERS.

BLESSED BE THE DIVINE GREEN GODDESS
SHE IS THE CREATRESS OF ALL LIVING THINGS.
BLESSED BE THE LORD OF THE GREENWOOD.
TO GODDESS AND GOD
THIS SONG I SING.

AWAKEN ONE, AWAKEN ALL
AND HEAR THE VOICE OF THE GODDESS CALL.
BLESSED BE OUR MOTHER EARTH,
MAY SHE BE FILLED WITH PEACE,
MAGICK, AND LOVE.

THE GODDESS BREATHES LIFE.
THE GODDESS GIVES LIFE.
THE GODDESS IS LIFE.
SHE REIGNS SUPREME.
SO MOTE IT BE!

End the rite by putting out the candle and uncasting the circle with the ceremonial sword in a counterclockwise motion.

The eggs may be eaten as part of a Spring Equinox Sabbat feast and the shells cast into an open fire or buried in the ground as an offering to the Earth Mother.

BELTANE SABBAT
May 1

The Witches' Sabbat of Beltane officially begins at moonrise on May Day Eve, and is traditionally performed high on a hilltop where the huge Beltane bonfires are lit to light the way for Summer and to increase fertility in animals, crops, and homes. (In the old days, the great bonfires of Ireland which symbolized the life-giving Sun God were kindled either by a spark from flint or by the friction of two sticks rubbing together.)

If you plan to celebrate the Beltane Sabbat indoors, a Beltane fire may be burned in a fireplace. (Be sure to hang a branch or twig from a rowan tree over the fire to honor the guardian spirits of your home and family, bring good luck into your home, and keep away all mischievous ghosts, elves, and fairy-folk.) If you do not have a fireplace, you may light thirteen dark green candles to symbolize the Beltane fire.

Dress in bright springtime colors (unless you prefer to work skyclad) and wear lots of colorful and fragrant flowers in your hair. (Before dressing for the ceremony, you should meditate and bathe by candlelight in an herbal bath to cleanse your body and soul of any impurities or negative energy.)

Begin by casting a circle about nine feet in diameter, and erect an altar in the middle of it, facing east. On top of the altar, in the center, place two small statues to represent the Goddess of Fertility and Her consort, the Horned God. On each side of the two statues, place a censer containing frankincense and Solomon's seal. On the right side of the altar, place a consecrated athame and a chalice filled with wine. Light thirteen dark green candles and place them around the circle.

Prepare a crown of springtime wildflowers such as daisies, primroses, yellow cowslips, or marigolds, and place it on the altar before the symbols of the Goddess and God.

A small Maypole (about three feet in height) may be erected at the right of the altar and decorated with flowers and brightly-colored ribbons.

Kneel before the altar. Light the altar candles and incense. Close your eyes, concentrate on the divine image of the Goddess and God, and say:

IN HONOR OF THE GODDESS AND HORNED GOD
AND UNDER THEIR PROTECTION
IS THIS SABBAT RITE NOW BEGUN.

Return to your feet. Take the athame from the altar, hold it out in salute toward the east, and say:

O GODDESS OF ALL THINGS WILD AND FREE
THIS CIRCLE I CONSECRATE TO THEE.

Hold your athame out in salute toward the south, and say:

BLESSED BE THE MAID OF SPRING
TO HER THIS PRAYER OF LOVE I SING.
SHE MAKES THE WOODS AND MEADOWS GREEN,
O GODDESS OF NATURE
SHE REIGNS SUPREME.

Hold your athame out in salute toward the west, and say:

FRANKINCENSE AND SOLOMON'S SEAL,
HAIL TO SHE WHO TURNS THE WHEEL!

Hold your athame out in salute toward the north, and say:

BLESSED BE THE LORD OF SPRING
TO HIM THE PRAYER OF LOVE I SING.
DIVINE GOD OF DARKNESS,
DIVINE GOD OF LIGHT,
HIS FERTILIZING POWERS
I CELEBRATE TONIGHT.

Return the athame to the top of the altar. Take the crown of wildflowers and place it on top of your head. (When this Sabbat ritual is performed by a coven, it is customary for the High Priest to place the crown of wildflowers upon the head of the High Priestess.) Kneel before the altar, facing the images of the Pagan fertility deities. Hold out your arms and say:

SPIRITS OF THE WATER AND AIR
I ASK THEE NOW TO HEAR MY PRAYER:
LET THE SKY AND SEA BE CLEAN
LET THE LAND BE FERTILE GREEN.
SPIRITS OF THE FIRE

SPIRITS OF THE MOTHER EARTH,
LET THE WORLD BE BLESSED
WITH PEACE, LOVE, AND MIRTH.

Raise the chalice of wine. Hold at arm's length and, as you pour a tiny bit of wine on the ground as a libation to the Goddess and Horned God, close your eyes and say:

SACRED BELTANE FIRES BURN,
LIGHT THE WAY FOR SUN'S RETURN.
WINTER'S DARKNESS NOW MUST END,
THE GREAT WHEEL OF LIFE
HAS TURNED AGAIN.
SO MOTE IT BE!

Drink the rest of the wine from the chalice, and then return it to the altar. Put out the candles, but allow the incense to burn itself out.

The ritual is now complete and should be followed by a joyous celebration of feasting, singing, and dancing sunwise around the Beltane bonfire or a decorated May-pole to symbolize the divine union of the Goddess and Her consort, the Horned God.

SUMMER SOLSTICE SABBAT
First Day of Summer

The following ritual is traditionally performed by Witches in a forest clearing, a large secluded garden, on a hilltop, or any other place of Nature.

Begin by arranging stones on the ground to form a large circle about nine feet in diameter. With a conse-crated ceremonial sword or long wooden stick (prefera-bly a freshly-cut rowan wand), draw the powerful and highly magickal symbol of a pentacle (five-pointed star) inside the stone circle. Light five green candles to symbolize the powers of Nature and fertility, and place one at each point of the pentagram, starting at the east point and continuing in a clockwise manner.

Erect an altar or lay a large, flat stone in the center of the pentagram facing north as an altar, and place on it a statue representing the Goddess. At each side of the statue, light a white altar candle. To the right (east), place a consecrated brass bell and a censer of frankincense and myrrh incense. To the left (west), place a chalice of wine, a small dish of salt, and a small bowl of water (preferably fresh rainwater).

Bless the wine by holding your palms down over the chalice as you say:

> I CONSECRATE AND BLESS THIS WINE
> IN THE DIVINE NAME OF THE GODDESS.

Sprinkle a bit of salt and a few drops of water over the brass bell to bless it, and say:

> WITH SALT AND WATER
> I CONSECRATE AND BLESS THIS BELL
> IN THE DIVINE NAME OF THE GODDESS.
> BLESSED BE.

Light the frankincense and myrrh. Raise your arms to the sky, close your eyes and fill your mind with pleasant thoughts and visions of the Mother Goddess as you say:

> O BLESSED EARTH MOTHER,
> WOMB-GODDESS, CREATRESS OF ALL,

THIS SACRED CIRCLE IS CONSECRATED
TO THEE.
IN YOUR SACRED NAME
AND UNDER YOUR PROTECTION
IS THIS SABBAT RITE NOW BEGUN.

Ring the bell thrice and invoke:

SACRED LADY-SPIRIT OF THE AIR
FIRE MAIDEN, BEAUTIFUL AND FAIR
EARTH MOTHER, GIVER OF LIVES,
CRONE OF WATER, AGELESS AND WISE,
I NOW CALL FORTH THY DIVINE IMAGE!

Return the bell to the stone altar and then, with both
hands, raise the chalice of wine to your lips. Drink some
of the wine and then pour the rest over the center of the
pentagram as a libation to the Goddess, as you say:

THIS BLESSED WINE I DO POUR
AS AN OFFERING TO THEE
O GRACIOUS GODDESS OF LOVE,
FERTILITY, AND LIFE.

Return the empty chalice to the altar. Again ring the
bell thrice and say:

WITH THE SUN IN ITS ZENITH
THIS SOLSTICE RITUAL I DO PERFORM
IN HONOR OF THEE, O GREAT GODDESS,
AND IN THY SACRED NAME
DO I NOW GIVE PRAISE.
AS THE DAYS OF SUNLIGHT BEGIN TO WANE
YOUR DIVINE LOVE AND HEALING POWERS
GROW STRONGER.

Kneel before the altar. Offer up more incense, ring the bell in praise of the Goddess, and then say in a loud and joyous tone of voice:

BLESSED BE THE GODDESS!
BLESSED BE THE GODDESS!

THE GODDESS IS LIFE.
THE GODDESS IS LOVE.
SHE TURNS THE GREAT SOLAR WHEEL
THAT CHANGES THE SEASONS
AND BRINGS NEW LIFE INTO THE WORLD.

BLESSED BE THE GODDESS!
BLESSED BE THE GODDESS!

THE GODDESS IS THE MOON AND STARS.
THE GODDESS IS THE SEA AND EARTH.
THE GODDESS IS THE CYCLE OF SEASONS.
SHE IS LIFE, SHE IS DEATH.
SHE IS RE-BIRTH.
SHE IS DAY, SHE IS NIGHT,
SHE IS DARKNESS, SHE IS LIGHT,
SHE IS ALL THINGS WILD AND FREE.
SO MOTE IT BE!

The Rite of the Summer Solstice should be followed by feasting, merriment, and the joyous singing of magickal Pagan folk songs and/or the recitation of Goddess-inspired poetry.

The Summer Solstice is the traditional time to harvest magickal herbs for spells and potions (especially those of love-magick!). It is also the ideal time to perform divinations and healing rituals, and to cut wands and divining rods.

LAMMAS SABBAT
August 1

Begin by casting a circle about nine feet in diameter. Erect an altar in the center of the circle, facing north. On the altar, place a candle of the appropriate Sabbat color. To the left (west) of the candle, place a chalice of water (preferably fresh rainwater or mountain spring water) and a fireproof tray or dish containing a new corn dolly and the one from last year's Lammas Sabbat. To the right (east) of the candle, place a censer of sandalwood or rose incense and a dish of salt, dirt, or sand to represent the element of earth. Before the candle (south), place a consecrated athame and a consecrated ceremonial sword.

Sprinkle a bit of salt to consecrate the circle, and then, starting in the east, trace the circle with the tip of the ceremonial sword, moving in a clockwise direction, and say:

WITH SALT AND SACRED SWORD
I CONSECRATE AND INVOKE THEE
O SABBAT CIRCLE OF MAGICK AND LIGHT.
IN THE SACRED NAME OF THE GODDESS
AND UNDER HER PROTECTION
IS THIS SABBAT RITE NOW BEGUN.

Return the ceremonial sword to the altar. Light the candle and say:

IN THIS CONSECRATED SABBAT CIRCLE
I NOW CONJURE THEE

O SACRED SPIRITS
OF THE ANCIENT AND MYSTICAL
ELEMENT OF FIRE.

Light the incense and say:

IN THIS CONSECRATED SABBAT CIRCLE
I NOW CONJURE THEE
O SACRED SPIRITS
OF THE ANCIENT AND MYSTICAL
ELEMENT OF AIR.

Take the athame in your right hand, and with the tip
of the blade draw a pentacle (five-pointed star) in the
salt, dirt, or sand, and say:

IN THIS CONSECRATED SABBAT CIRCLE
I NOW CONJURE THEE
O SACRED SPIRITS
OF THE ANCIENT AND MYSTICAL
ELEMENT OF EARTH.

Dip the blade of the athame into the chalice of water,
and say:

IN THIS CONSECRATED SABBAT CIRCLE
I NOW CONJURE THEE
O SACRED SPIRITS
OF THE ANCIENT AND MYSTICAL
ELEMENT OF WATER

Return the athame to the altar. Take the new corn
dolly and place it to the right of the candle, and say:

O LADY OF THE HARVEST
I GIVE THEE THANKS

FOR SUSTAINING US
IN THE SEASONS TO COME
BY THE BOUNTY OF THIS HARVEST.
SO MOTE IT BE.

Take the old corn dolly and light it with the flame of the candle. Place it in the fireproof tray or dish. As it burns, recite the following magickal Sabbat rhyme:

LADY OF HARVEST PAST, NOW BURN.
TO THE GODDESS YE SHALL RETURN.
BLESS ME WITH THE LUCK AND LOVE
OF GOD AND GODDESS UP ABOVE.
SO MOTE IT BE!

End the rite by dismissing the elemental spirits, extinguishing the candle, and uncasting the circle in a counterclockwise direction with the ceremonial sword.

Bury the ashes of the old corn dolly as an offering to the Earth Mother, and save the new corn dolly for the next Lammas Sabbat.

AUTUMN EQUINOX SABBAT
First Day of Fall

Begin by casting a circle about nine feet in diameter. In the center, erect an altar facing north. On the altar, place a candle of the appropriate Sabbat color, a chalice of water, an athame, a dish of salt, dirt, or sand, a consecrated altar bell, and a censer of incense. (The following incenses are sacred on this Sabbat: benzoin, myrrh, passionflower, red poppies, and sage.)

Decorate the altar with traditional holiday decorations such as acorns, pinecones, marigolds, white roses, and thistles. The flowers can be arranged in bouquets or garlands for the altar or circle, or made into a crown and worn on top of the head.

Sprinkle a bit of salt inside the circle, and then trace the circle with a consecrated ceremonial sword or wand, and say:

WITH SALT AND SACRED SWORD
I CONSECRATE AND CAST THIS SABBAT CIRCLE.
IN THE DIVINE NAME OF THE GODDESS
AND UNDER HER PROTECTION
IS THIS SABBAT RITE NOW BEGUN.

Light the candle and incense. Ring the altar bell thrice with your left hand to begin the Equinox Rite and conjuration of the elemental spirits. Take the athame in your right hand, face the east, and say:

O SACRED SYLPHS OF THE AIR
AND ELEMENTAL KINGS OF THE EAST
I CONJURE THEE AND BID THEE TO
COME AND PARTAKE IN THIS SABBAT RITE
IN THIS CONSECRATED CIRCLE.

Face the south, and say:

O SACRED SALAMANDERS OF THE FIRE
AND ELEMENTAL KINGS OF THE SOUTH
I CONJURE THEE AND BID THEE TO
COME AND PARTAKE IN THIS SABBAT RITE
IN THIS CONSECRATED CIRCLE.

Face the west, and say:

O SACRED UNDINES OF THE WATER
AND ELEMENTAL KINGS OF THE WEST

I CONJURE THEE AND BID THEE TO
COME AND PARTAKE IN THIS SABBAT RITE
IN THIS CONSECRATED CIRCLE.

Face the north, and say:

O SACRED GNOMES OF THE EARTH
AND ELEMENTAL KINGS OF THE NORTH
I CONJURE THEE AND BID THEE TO
COME AND PARTAKE IN THIS SABBAT RITE
IN THIS CONSECRATED CIRCLE.

Ring the altar bell thrice and then return it to the altar. Stretch out your right arm and point the tip of the athame up to the heavens, and say:

AIR, FIRE, WATER, EARTH,
WOMB TO LIFE, DEATH TO REBIRTH.
THE GREAT WHEEL OF THE SEASONS TURNS,
THE SACRED SABBAT FIRE BURNS.
WE ARE ALL CHILDREN OF THE GODDESS
AND TO HER WE SHALL RETURN.

Dip the blade of the athame into the chalice of water, and then into the dish of salt, dirt, or sand, and say:

BLESSED BE THE GODDESS OF LOVE,
CREATRESS OF ALL THINGS WILD AND FREE.
THE WARMTH OF SUMMER
NOW MUST END.
THE GREAT SOLAR WHEEL
HAS TURNED AGAIN
SO MOTE IT BE!

Ring the altar bell thrice to end the rite, dismiss the

elemental spirits, and give thanks to the Goddess. Then uncast the circle in a counterclockwise manner with the ceremonial sword or wand.

SAMHAIN SABBAT
October 31

In many Wiccan traditions, it is customary for a Witch to fast for a whole day before performing the Samhain Sabbat Ritual.

After a ritual bath in salt water to cleanse your body and soul of any impurities and negative energy, put on a long, black ceremonial robe (unless you prefer to work skyclad, as many Witches do), wear a handcrafted necklace of acorns around your neck, and place a crown of oak leaves around your head.

Begin by casting a circle about nine feet in diameter, using white chalk or paint. Place thirteen black and orange candles around the circle, and as you light each one, say:

SAMHAIN CANDLE OF FIRE SO BRIGHT
CONSECRATE THIS CIRCLE OF LIGHT.

In the center of the circle, erect an altar facing north. On the center of the altar, place three candles (one white, one red, and one black) to represent each phase of the Triple Goddess. To the left (west) of the candles, place a chalice filled with apple cider and a dish containing sea salt. To the right (east) of the candles, place a censer of herb incense and a small bowl of water. Before the candles (south), place a brass altar bell, a consecrated athame, and a red apple.

Ring the altar bell thrice, and say:

> IN THE SACRED NAME OF THE GODDESS
> AND UNDER HER PROTECTION
> IS THIS SABBAT RITE NOW BEGUN.

Sprinkle a bit of salt and water at each compass point around the circle to cleanse the space of any negativity or evil influences. Take the athame in your right hand, and say:

> HEARKEN WELL YE ELEMENTS
> AIR, FIRE, WATER, EARTH
> BY BELL AND BLADE I SUMMON THEE
> ON THIS SACRED NIGHT OF MIRTH.

Dip the blade of the athame into the chalice of apple cider, and say:

> I OFFER TO THEE, O GODDESS
> THIS NECTAR OF THE SEASON.

Return the athame to the altar. Light the incense and the three altar candles, and say:

> THREE CANDLES I DO LIGHT
> IN HONOR OF THEE, O GODDESS:
> WHITE FOR THE MAIDEN,
> RED FOR THE MOTHER,
> BLACK FOR THE CRONE.
>
> O GODDESS OF ALL THINGS WILD AND FREE,
> STRONG AND LOVING, FAIR AND JUST,
> THIS SACRED TEMPLE I RAISE TO THEE
> IN PERFECT LOVE,
> IN PERFECT TRUST.

Pick up the chalice with both hands and pour a few drops of the cider onto the apple, and say:

TO THE WOMB OF THE MOTHER GODDESS
THE HORNED GOD NOW RETURNS
UNTIL THE DAY WHEN HE IS REBORN AGAIN.
THE GREAT SOLAR WHEEL
ONCE AGAIN TURNS.
THE CYCLE OF THE SEASONS NEVER ENDS.

BLESSED BE THE SOULS OF THOSE
WHO HAVE JOURNEYED BEYOND
TO THE DARK WORLD OF THE DEAD.
I POUR THIS NECTAR
IN HONOR OF THEIR MEMORY.
MAY THE GODDESS BLESS THEM
WITH LIGHT, BEAUTY, AND JOY
BLESSED BE!
BLESSED BE!

Drink the remaining cider, and then return the chalice to its place on the altar. Ring the bell thrice, and then uncast the circle by extinguishing the orange and black candles, starting at the east and moving in a counterclockwise direction.

Take the apple from the altar and bury it outside in the earth to nourish the souls of those who have died in the past year.

The Samhain Ritual is now complete and should be followed by meditation, divination by crystal ball, the reciting of mystical Goddess-inspired poetry, and a Witches' prayer for the souls of all family members and friends who have passed on to the Spiritual Plane.

WINTER SOLSTICE SABBAT
First Day of Winter

Begin by erecting an altar, facing north. Around it, cast a circle about nine feet in diameter using white chalk or paint. Decorate the altar with holly, mistletoe, or any other herb sacred on this Sabbat.

Place a white altar candle on the center of the altar. To the left of the candle, place a chalice of red wine or apple cider and a censer of incense. (Any of the following incense fragrances are appropriate for this ritual: bay, cedar, pine, or rosemary.) To the right of the candle, place a consecrated athame and a dish of salt. Behind the altar, place an oak Yule log with thirteen green and red candles affixed to it.

Take the athame in your right hand and scoop up a bit of salt with the tip of the blade. Drop the salt from the athame into the circle. Repeat three times and say:

> BLESSED BE THIS SACRED SABBAT CIRCLE
> IN THE NAME OF THE GREAT HORNED
>   GOD
> THE DIVINE LORD OF DARKNESS AND
>   LIGHT
> THE GOD OF DEATH AND ALL THAT
>   COMES AFTER.
> BLESSED BE THIS SACRED SABBAT CIRCLE
> IN HIS NAME.

Return the athame to its place on the altar. After lighting the incense and candle, once again take the athame in your right hand. Dip the blade into the chalice and say:

> O GREAT GODDESS
> EARTH MOTHER OF ALL LIVING THINGS,
> WE BID THEE FAREWELL
> AS YE NOW GO TO REST.
> BLESSED BE!
>
> AND WE WELCOME THEE

O GREAT HORNED GOD OF THE HUNT,
EARTH FATHER OF ALL LIVING THINGS.
BLESSED BE!

WATER, AIR, FIRE, EARTH,
WE CELEBRATE THE SUN'S REBIRTH.
ON THIS DARK AND LONGEST NIGHT
WE BURN THE SACRED CANDLES
   BRIGHT.

Return the athame to the altar. Pick up the chalice
with both hands, and as you raise it to your lips, say:

THIS WINE I DRINK TO HONOR THEE
O GOD OF ALL THINGS WILD AND FREE.
WE THANK THEE FOR THE LIGHT OF THE SUN.
HAIL TO THEE, O GREAT HORNED ONE!

Drink the wine, and then return the chalice to its
place on the altar.

Light the thirteen candles on the Yule log, and end
the Winter Solstice Rite by saying:

THE SACRED YULE LOG FIRE BURNS,
THE GREAT SOLAR WHEEL ONCE AGAIN TURNS.
SO MOTE IT BE!

Celebrate merrily and feast with family and friends
until the last candle on the Yule log burns itself out.

5

The Art of Magick

The practice of magick is ancient in its origin and is found the world over.

Magick is a force that combines psychic energy with the powers of the will to produce "supernatural" effects, cause change to occur in conformity, and control events in Nature. It increases the flow of divinity, and can be used for constructive purposes as well as destructive ones.

Magick is a neutral force that in itself is neither good nor evil. The direction of good or evil is determined by the practitioner. However, as threefold karma is returned to all for their actions in this lifetime, it would be an act of self-destruction for any Witch or magician to use black magick to bring harm upon another.

As a tool of Wicca Craft, the old spelling of the word "magick" with the "k" at the end is often used by Witches to distinguish it from the non-Craft magic of theatrical stage conjuring, sleight of hand, and illusion.

Magick is a powerful tool. It is an important part of Wicca, although secondary to the worship of the Goddess and Her consort, the Horned God.

One of the most important elements in the practice of magick is feeling. It is absolutely essential that you possess strong feelings about what you are attempting to accomplish in order to produce the power needed to perform magick.

It is also very important to use creative visualization, also known as "willed imagination." This is the magickal art or skill of imagining the end results of your magick in order to make your desires materialize. It is a natural, Goddess-given ability in certain people; however, most of us need to activate and cultivate our powers through lots of practice, concentration exercises, and meditation. When spellcasting, always concentrate deeply and fill your mind with a clear mental picture of what it is that you want or need.

Without feeling and creative visualization, it is extremely difficult (if not absolutely impossible) for magick to work.

You will also find that better results are achieved if you work spells yourself and/or create your own amulets, talismans, and potions, rather than rely upon someone else (especially a stranger) to perform the magick for you. When you perform a spell for yourself, you empower the magick with your own emotional, spiritual, and psychic vibrations.

Use magick wisely, cautiously, and *only* in a positive way. All magick is serious business and should never be abused or treated as a parlor game or as a joke. Never use any form of magick to manipulate another person's will or emotions, and always keep in mind the Wiccan Rede which states: AN IT HARM NONE, DO WHAT THOU WILT. Black magick will not only bring you threefold bad karma, it will also backfire and bring you disastrous results.

Before performing magick, it is always wise to do a divination of some kind to find out whether the results of your magick will be positive or negative. You can use a crystal ball, tarot cards, candles, rune stones, or whatever method you prefer to use. If you are not skilled in the art of divination, consult an experienced Witch or a reputable master of the occult arts.

Magick is powerful and it works; however, certain spells may have to be repeated several times until you get them right, especially if you are new to magick. Don't be discouraged by failure. With enough training and practice, you will soon get a "feel" for magick and be able to use its powers to work for you.

Just as there are many different Wiccan traditions, magick also takes many different forms. There is ceremonial magick, Kabbalistic magick, Native American magick (also known as Shamanism), Vodoun magick, and many more. Choosing the right form (or forms) of magick to practice depends entirely upon a Witch's personal preference and/or Wiccan tradition, although many Wiccans choose to practice European-influenced folk magick.

Some Witches devote their entire lives to the study and practice of only one form of magick, while others experiment and practice different types. It is entirely up to the individual.

Magick is the science of the secrets of Nature, and in order to work it properly, a Witch must always work in perfect harmony with the laws of Nature and the psyche. Bathing in salted water and cleansing the inner body by fasting for a whole day before performing a magick ritual is often necessary, especially in ceremonial magick. To be able to produce power, the physical body must be kept in a healthy condition.

The moon and each of its phases are the most essential part of magick, and it is extremely important that spells and rituals be performed during the proper lunar phase.

A waxing moon (the time from the new moon through the first quarter to the full moon) is the proper time to perform positive magick and spells that increase love, good luck, sexual desire, and wealth.

A full moon increases extrasensory perception, and is the proper time to perform lunar Goddess invocations, fertility rituals, and spells that increase psychic abilities and prophetic dreams.

A waning moon (the time from the full moon through the last quarter to the new moon) is the proper time to perform destructive magick, negative incantations, and spells that remove curses, hexes, and jinxes, end bad relationships, reverse love spells and aphrodisiacs, break bad habits, and decrease fevers, pains, and sickness.

Summing up, to perform successful magick, one must be in harmony with the laws of Nature and the psyche. It is important to possess magickal knowledge, a healthy body and mind, and the ability to accept responsibility for one's own actions. It is impossible to magickally obtain positive results if you have a low energy level, or contaminate your system with harmful drugs and/or excessive amounts of alcohol. Working

e proper lunar phase, conviction, concentra-
visualization of the end result are all the secrets of successful magick!

PLANETARY RULERS AND RITUAL
INFLUENCES OF THE DAYS OF THE WEEK

SUNDAY: (ruled by the Sun) is the proper day of the
week to perform spells and rituals involving exor-
cism, healing, and prosperity. *Colors*: orange, white,
yellow. *Incense*: lemon, frankincense.

MONDAY: (ruled by the Moon) is the proper day of
the week to perform spells and rituals involving agriculture, animals, female fertility, messages, recon-
ciliations, theft, and voyages. *Colors*: silver, white,
gray. *Incense*: African violet, honeysuckle, myrtle,
willow, wormwood.

TUESDAY: (ruled by Mars) is the proper day of the
week to perform spells and rituals involving courage,
physical strength, revenge, military honors, surgery,
and the breaking of negative spells. *Colors*: red, orange. *Incense*: dragon's blood, patchouli.

WEDNESDAY: (ruled by Mercury) is the proper day of
the week to perform spells and rituals involving communication, divination, writing, knowledge, and
business transactions. *Colors*: yellow, gray, violet,
and all opalescent hues. *Incense*: jasmine, lavender,
sweetpea.

THURSDAY: (ruled by Jupiter) is the proper day of the
week to perform spells and rituals involving luck,
happiness, health, legal matters, male fertility, treasure, and wealth. *Colors*: blue, purple, indigo. *Incense*:
cinnamon, musk, nutmeg, sage.

FRIDAY: (ruled by Venus) is the proper day of the
week to perform spells and rituals involving love,
romance, marriage, sexual matters, physical beauty,

friendships, and partnerships. *Colors*: pink, green, aqua, chartreuse. *Incense*: strawberry, sandalwood, rose, saffron, vanilla.

SATURDAY: (ruled by Saturn) is the proper day of the week to perform spells and rituals involving spirit communication, meditation, psychic attack or defense, and locating lost things and missing persons. *Colors*: black, gray, indigo. *Incense*: black poppy seeds, myrrh.

CHARMS

Although the word "charm" is often used to describe an amulet or talisman, a charm is actually a magickal song or incantation which is sung or recited as a spell, or chanted over an amulet or talisman to consecrate it and charge it with magickal energy.

The use of charms is common among shamans in many parts of the world, especially in South America where magickal chants accompany nearly every magickal rite.

Charms are usually used to avert impending dangers, expel diseases, summon spirits, and ensure good luck.

A countercharm is a powerful magickal chant, amulet, or talisman which is used to neutralize or reverse the effects of another charm or spell.

AMULETS

An amulet is a consecrated object (usually a small, colored stone, a gemstone, or part of a plant) which is magickally charged with power to draw love or good luck. Amulets, like charms and talismans, can also be used to stimulate good health, avert danger, and protect against negative influences such as the Evil Eye.

Love amulets (commonly called "love charms") are

used by Witches as magickal tools to inspire love and romance, reunite parted lovers, attract a spouse, prevent a love affair from breaking up, and so on. Almost anything can be used as an amulet: a brightly-colored gemstone, a religious figurine, a root, a flower, or a bone. Amulets can be carried in the hand or in a pocket, worn as jewelry, buried in the earth, or secretly placed somewhere within a house, a barn, or even an automobile. Amulets can be bought, found, or made by hand. They can also be painted or inscribed with magickal words of power and/or symbols to attract certain influences.

The use of amulets is universal among nearly every culture, and is familiar to most modern-day Americans and Europeans in the form of the lucky rabbit's foot, four-leaf clovers, horseshoes, birthstone rings, and lucky pennies.

Another type of amulet is the charm bag: a small leather, silk, or flannel pocket filled with various magickal things, and worn or carried for protection or attraction.

A charm bag filled with magickal herbs, leaves, flowers, or roots is known as an "herbal love amulet" or a "Witch's sachet." Charm bags used in love magick are called "love bags" or "mojos." In the southern region of the United States, they are known as "hoodoo hands," "tricks," and "tricken bags." The Native Americans call them "medicine bundles," and in Africa they are given the name "gris-gris."

TALISMANS

A talisman is a man-made object of any shape or material, charged with magickal properties to bring good luck or fertility, and to ward off negativity.

To formally charge a talisman with power, it must first be inscribed and then consecrated. Inscribing the talisman with a sun sign, moon sign, birthdate, astrological sign, runic name, or other magickal symbol personalizes it and gives it purpose.

The most famous of all magickal talismans is the Abracadabra Triangle which, in ancient times, was believed to possess the power to ward off illness and cure fever when its letters were arranged in an inverted pyramid (a holy figure and symbol of trinity) on a piece of parchment, worn around the neck with flax for nine days and nights, and then thrown backwards over the left shoulder into a stream flowing to the east. (Abracadabra is said to be a cabalistic word derived from the name "Abraxas," a mighty Gnostic deity whose name means "hurt me not.")

In Abramelin magick, powerful magickal talismans known as "magick squares" are made from rows of numbers or letters of the alphabet arranged so that the words may read horizontally or vertically as palindromes, and the numbers total the same when added up in either direction.

In order for a magick number square to work properly, it must include every consecutive number from one until the square is filled, and according to the rules of numerology, each number can only be used once in a square.

MAGICK WORD SQUARES

To make visions appear in magick mirrors or crystal balls, inscribe the following gnomotic square on a piece of consecrated parchment and place it under the glass or crystal:

```
G  I  L  I  O  N  I  N
I                    I
L                    N
I                    O
O                    I
N                    L
I                    I
N  I  N  O  I  L  I  G
```

To protect against bewitchment, lift hexes, and ward off the powers of the Evil Eye, inscribe the following square on a piece of consecrated parchment and wear it on a white string around your neck:

```
L  A  C  H  A  T
A              A
C              H
H              C
A              A
T  A  H  C  A  L
```

To make a spirit appear before you in human form, inscribe the following words of power on a square piece of consecrated parchment, and then take the symbol in your right hand and thrice say out loud the name of the spirit whom you wish to summon:

L	E	V	I	A	T	A	N
E	R	M	O	G	A	S	A
V	M	I	R	T	E	A	T
I	O	R	A	N	T	G	A
A	G	T	N	A	R	O	I
T	A	E	T	R	I	M	V
A	S	A	G	O	M	R	E
N	A	T	A	I	V	E	L

6

Pagan Deities

Different Pagan deities should be invoked for spells and rituals involving particular subjects. The following is a list of subjects and their corresponding deities.

AGRICULTURE: Adonis, Amon, Aristaeus, Baldur, Bonus Eventus, Ceres, Consus, Dagon, Demeter, Dumuzi, Esus, Ghanan, Inari, Osiris, Saturn, Tammuz, Thor, Triptolemus, Vertumnus, Xochipilli, Yumcaax.
THE ARTS: Ea, Hathor, Odin, Thene, Thor.
ASTROLOGY: Albion.
CATS: Bast, Freya.

CHILDBIRTH: Althea, Bes, Carmenta, Cihuatcoatl, Cuchavira, Isis, Kuan Yin, Laima, Lucina, Meshkent.
COMMUNICATIONS: Hermes, Hermod, Janus, Mercury.
COURAGE: Tyr.
DREAMS: Geshtinanna, Morpheus, Nanshe.
THE EARTH: Asia, Consus, Daghda, Enlil, Frigga, Frija, Gaea, Ge, Geb, Kronos, Ninhursag, Ops, Prithivi, Rhea, Saturn, Sif, Tellus.
FERTILITY: Amun, Anaitis, Apollo, Arrianrhod, Asherali, Astarte, Attis, Baal, Bacchus, Bast, Bona Dea, Boucca, Centeotle, Cernunnos, Cerridwen, Cybele, Daghda, Demeter, Dew, Dionysus, Eostre, Frey, Freya, Frigga, Indra, Ishtar, Ishwara, Isis, Kronos, Lono, Lupercus, Min, Mut, Mylitta, Ningirsu, Ops, Osiris, Ostara, Oya, Pan, Pomona, Quetzalcoatl, Rhea, Rhiannon, Saturn, Selkhet, Sida, Tane, Telepinu, Telluno, Tellus Mater, Thunor, Tlazolteotl, Yarilo, Zarpanitu.
GOOD LUCK AND FORTUNE: Bonus Eventus, Daikoku, Fortuna, Ganesa, Jorojin, Laima, Tyche.
HEALING: Apollo, Asclepius, Bast, Brigid, Eira, Gula, Ixtlilton, Khons, Paeon.
JOURNEYS: Echua, Janus, Min.
LAW, TRUTH, AND JUSTICE: Astraea, Maat, Misharu, Themis.
LOVE: Aizen Myo-o, Alpan, Angus, Aphrodite, Asera, Astarte, Asthoreth, Belili, Creirwy, Cupid, Dzydzilelya, Erato, Eros, Erzulie, Esmeralda, Februa, Freya, Frigga, Habondia, Hathor, Inanna, Ishtar, Kades, Kama, Kivan-Non, Kubaba, Melusine, Menu, Minne, Nanaja, Odudua, Olwen, Oshun, Prenda, Sauska, Tlazolteotl, Turan, Venus, Xochipilli, Xochiquetzal.

LUNAR MAGICK: Aah, Artemis, Asherali, Astarte, Baiame, Bendis, Diana, Gou, Hathor, Hecate, Ilmaqah, Ishtar, Isis, Jacy, Kabul, Khons, Kilya, Lucina, Luna, Mah, Mama Quilla, Mani, Menu, Metzli, Myestas, Nanna, Pah, Selene, Sin, Soma, Taukiyomi, Thoth, Varuna, Yarikh, Yerak, Zamna.

MARRIAGE: Airyaman, Aphrodite, Aryaman, Bes, Bhaga, Ceres, Erato, Frigga, Hathor, Hera, Hymen, Juno, Pattini, Salacia, Svarog, Thalassa, Tutunis, Vor, Xochipilli.

MUSIC AND/OR POETRY: Apollo, Benten, Bragi, Brigid, Hathor, Orpheus, Odin, Thoth, Vainemuine, Woden, Xochipilli.

PROPHECY, DIVINATION, AND THE MAGICKAL ARTS: Anubis, Apollo, Brigid, Carmenta, Ea, Exu, Hecate, Isis, Odin, Set, Shamash, Simbi, Tages, Thoth, Untunktahe, Woden, Xolotl.

REINCARNATION: Hera, Khensu, Ra.

THE SEA: Amphitrite, Benten, Dylan, Ea, Enoil, Glaucus, Leucothea, Manannan Mac Lir, Neptune, Nereus, Njord, Paldemon, Phorcys, Pontus, Poseidon, Proteus, Shoney, Yamm.

THE SKY: Aditi, Anshar, Anu, Dyaus, Frigg, Hathor, Horus, Joch-Huva, Jupiter, Kumarbis, Nut, Obatala, Rangi, Svarog, Tane, Thor, Tiwaz, Ukko, Uranus, Varuna, Zeus.

SHAPESHIFTING: Freya, Volkh, Xolotl, Zeus.

SLEEP: Hypnos. (See also the Pagan deities who preside over *DREAMS.*)

SOLAR MAGICK: Amaterasu, Apollo, Atum, Baldur, Bochica, Dazhbog, Helios, Hiruko, Horus, Hyperion, Inti, Legba, Lugh, Mandulis, Mao, Marduk, Maui, Melkart, Mithra, Orunjan, Paiva, Perun, Phoebus, Ra, Sabazius, Samas, Sams, Shamash, Sol, Surya,

Tezcatlipoca, Tonatiuh, Torushompek, Utto, Vishnu, Yhi.

VENGEANCE: Nemesis.

WEALTH AND PROSPERITY: Daikoku, Jambhala, Kubera, Plutus, Thor.

WEATHERWORKING: Adad, Aeolus, Agni, Amen, Baal, Bragi, Buriash, Catequil, Chac-Mool, Chernobog, Donar, Fomagata, Ilyapa, Indra, Jove, Jupiter, Kami-Nari, Koza, Lei-Kung, Marduk, Nyame, Perkunas, Pillan, Pulug, Quiateot, Raiden, Rammon, Rudra, Shango, Sobo, Summanus, Taki-Tsu-Hiko, Tawhaki, Tawhiri, Tefnut, Thor, Thunor, Tilo, Tinia, Typhoeus, Typhon, Yu-Tzu, Zeus, Zu.

WISDOM: Aruna, Athena, Atri, Baldur, Brigid, Dainichi, Ea, Enki, Fudo-Myoo, Fugen Bosatsu, Fukurokuju, Ganesa, Minerva, Nebo, Nimir, Oannes, Odin, Oghma, Quetzalcoatl, Sia, Sin, Thoth, Vohumano, Zeus.

7

Wortcunning

THE HISTORY OF HERBS

Herbs have been used to heal the body since prehistoric times, and the study of medicinal herbs dates back more than five thousand years to the ancient Sumerians.

Herbal remedies are a mainstay of traditional Chinese medicine, and the oldest known herb book is the Chinese *Pen–ts'ao* (Herbal) written by the Emperor Shennung (3737–2697 B.C.). Recorded in this book are over three hundred medicinal herb preparations.

The ancient Egyptians also used herbal remedies, and according to an ancient record called the Ebers Papyrus, there were nearly two thousand herb doctors practicing in Egypt around the year 2000 B.C.

Herbals were produced by the ancient Greeks, who studied the medicinal qualities of herbs and recorded their observations. According to the Greek philosopher, botanist, and author Theophrastus, more than three hundred medicinal herbs were grown in the garden of Aristotle.

In the first century A.D., the first European treatise on the properties and medicinal uses of herbs was compiled by Dioscorides, a Greek physician.

Herbal healing was an important rite in many pre-Christian religions. Repeated references to herbs appear even in the Old and New Testaments of the Bible, despite the fact that the early Christian church preferred faith healing to the formal practice of medicine, which they attempted to ban.

The Indian tribes of North America used herbs in both healing and the practice of magick, and found a use for nearly every plant native to their land. Their invaluable knowledge of many botanical medicines was passed along to the white European settlers in the United States and Canada.

In the year 1526, the anonymous *Grete Herball* was the first herbal to the published in the English language. In 1597, one of the most famous herbals of that era appeared. It was called *Gerard's Herball* and was the work of John Gerard, an English surgeon and apothecary to King James I. In 1640, John Parkinson's herbal *Theatrum Botanicum* was produced, followed by the astrologically-influenced herbal of Nicholas Culpepper.

As chemistry and other physical sciences rapidly developed in the eighteenth and nineteenth centuries, herbal medicine lost its popularity in the United States and Europe to active chemical drugs and the practice of chemotherapy.

In the United States today, there is a resurgence of

popular interest in herbs and herbal products, and some people (including Wiccans, New Agers, and back-to-nature folks) are beginning to turn away from the artificially-prepared medicines of modern society to seek out more natural and old-fashioned methods of healing.

Herbs are natural. Many can aid in preventing, as well as healing, diseases. And for many illnesses, Mother Nature's cures can be far better to use than unpleasant-tasting, man-made pills that are synthetic and temporarily relieve the symptoms but do not eradicate the cause of the illness.

(PLEASE NOTE: Many modern diseases call for modern methods of treatment. In the event of serious or chronic physical or emotional conditions, it is recommended that professional medical treatment be sought immediately.)

Many Wiccans enjoy growing their own herb gardens; however, most medicinal (and magickal) herbs can also be obtained at health food stores, herb farms, supermarkets, and even in the woods or along the roadside, if you know what you're looking for. (CAUTION: Many herbs are poisonous and can cause mild to severe sickness and, in some cases, even death. You should *never* attempt to gather wild herbs for medicinal use unless you are an herb expert or are accompanied by someone who is a trained, experienced herbalist.)

The more esoteric herbs can usually be obtained in occult shops or through mail order Witchcraft supply catalogues. (See my book, *The Magick of Candleburning*, for an up-to-date alphabetical list of mail order herb suppliers.)

TRADITIONAL RITUAL HERBS
OF THE SABBATS

CANDLEMAS SABBAT: angelica, basil, bay, benzoin, celandine, heather, myrrh, and all yellow flowers.

SPRING EQUINOX SABBAT: acorn, celandine, cinquefoil, crocus, daffodil, dogwood, Easter lily, honeysuckle, iris, jasmine, rose, strawberry, tansy, and violets.

BELTANE SABBAT: almond, angelica, ash tree, bluebells, cinquefoil, daisy, frankincense, hawthorn, ivy, lilac, marigold, meadowsweet, primrose, roses, satyrion root, woodruff, and yellow cowslips.

SUMMER SOLSTICE SABBAT: chamomile, cinquefoil, elder, fennel, hemp, larkspur, lavender, male fern, mugwort, pine, roses, Saint John's wort, wild thyme, wisteria, and verbena.

LAMMAS SABBAT: acacia flowers, aloes, cornstalks, cyclamen, fenugreek, frankincense, heather, hollyhock, myrtle, oak leaves, sunflower, and wheat.

AUTUMN EQUINOX SABBAT: acorns, asters, benzoin, ferns, honeysuckle, marigold, milkweed, mums, myrrh, oak leaves, passionflower, pine, roses, sage, Solomon's seal, and thistles.

SAMHAIN SABBAT: acorns, broom, apples, deadly nightshade, dittany, ferns, flax, fumitory, heather, mullein, oak leaves, pumpkins, sage, and straw.

WINTER SOLSTICE SABBAT: bay, bayberry, blessed thistle, cedar, chamomile, evergreen, frankincense, holly, juniper, mistletoe, moss, oak, pine cones, rosemary, and sage.

LUNAR HERB GARDENING

An increasing number of Witches are cultivating their own herbs, and whether it be an herb farm, a small garden in the backyard, or just a few flower pots on the kitchen windowsill, favorable results are always obtained when the herbs are planted in harmony with Mother Nature.

The phase of the moon and the sign of the zodiac the moon is in when the herb is planted are extremely important. Most herbs should be planted during a new or half moon in the sign of Cancer, Pisces, or Scorpio.

The exceptions are as follows:

GARLIC: Plant during a new or half moon in the sign of Scorpio or Sagittarius.

PARSLEY: Plant during a new moon in the sign of Pisces, Cancer, Libra, or Scorpio.

SAGE: Plant during a full moon in the sign of Pisces, Scorpio, or Cancer.

VALERIAN: Plant during a new or half moon in the sign of Gemini or Virgo.

Compost should be started when the waning moon is in the sign of Cancer, Pisces, or Scorpio.

Cultivation should begin when the waning moon is in Aquarius, Aries, Gemini, Leo, or Virgo.

The best time for fertilizing or transplanting is when the waxing moon is in Cancer, Pisces, or Scorpio.

Always consult an up-to-date lunar calendar before planting herbs, and avoid planting on the first day of the new moon or on the day when it increases to a half moon.

HERBS OF THE GODS

The following herbs are sacred to the gods and goddesses listed after them.

ACACIA: Al-Ozza, Buddha, Neith, and Osiris.
ACONITE: Hecate and Medea.
AGAVE: Mayauel.
ALL-HEAL: Hercules.
ANEMONE: Adonis, Aphrodite, and Venus.
ANGELICA: Atlantis and Michael.
ANISE: Apollo and Mercury.
ASTER: All Pagan gods and goddesses.
AZALEA: Hecate.
BARLEY: Odin.
BASIL: Erzulie, Krishna, Lakshmi, and Vishnu.
BELLADONNA: Atropos, Bellona, Circe, and Hecate.
BENZOIN: Aphrodite, Mut, and Venus.
BLACKTHORN: The Triple Goddess in Her dark and protective aspect.
BLESSED THISTLE: Pan.
BROOM: Blodeuwedd.
CAMPION: Aphrodite and Venus.
CATNIP: Bast and Sekhmet.
CENTAURY: The centaur Chiron.
CHAMOMILE: Karnayna.
CHASTE TREE: Ceres.
COLTSFOOT: Epona.
CORNFLOWER: Flora, and associated with the myths of Cyanus and Chiron.
COWSLIP: Freya.
CROCUS: Aphrodite and Venus.
DAFFODIL: Proserpina.
DAISY: Aphrodite, Artemis, Belides, Freya, Thor, Ve-

nus, Zeus, and associated with Mary Magdalene, Saint John, and Saint Margaret of Antioch.

DANDELION: Brigit.

DITTANY: Diana, Osiris, and Persephone.

DOGWOOD: Consus.

ELECAMPANE: Helen.

EYEBRIGHT: Euphrosyne.

FENNEL: Adonis.

FENUGREEK: Apollo.

FERNS: Kupala.

FLAX: Hulda.

GARLIC: Hecate and Mars.

HAWTHORN: Hymen.

HEATHER: Isis and Venus Erycina.

HELIOTROPE: Apollo, Helios, Ra, Sol, and all Sun Gods.

HOLLY: Hel, Mother Holle, and the Horned God in his waning year aspects.

HOREHOUND: Horus.

HOUSELEEK: Jupiter and Thor.

HYACINTH: Apollo, Artemis, and Hyacinthus.

IRIS: Hera, Horus, Iris, and Isis.

IVY: Attis, Bacchus, Dionysus, Dusares, and Osiris.

JASMINE: Diana.

JIMSONWEED: Apollo, Chingichnich, and Kwawar.

LADY'S MANTLE: Various Earth Goddesses, and associated with the Virgin Mary of the Christian mythos.

LAVENDER: Hecate, Saturn, and Vesta.

LETTUCE: Adonis.

LILY: Astarte, Hera, Juno, Lilith, and Ostara.

LOOSESTRIFE: Kupala.

LOTUS: Brahma, Buddha, Cunti, Hermes, Horus, Isis, Juno, Kuan-Yin, Lakshmi, Osiris, Padma, Tara, and associated with the myth of Lotis and Priapus.

MAIDENHAIR FERN: Dis, Kupala, and Venus.

MANDRAKE: Aphrodite, Diana, Hecate, Saturn, and associated with Circe and the legendary Teutonic sorceress, the Alrauna Maiden.

MARIGOLD: Xochiquetzal.

MARJORAM: Aphrodite and Venus.

MEADOWSWEET: Blodeuwedd.

MINTS: Dis, Hecate, Mintha, and associated with the classical legend of the nymph Menthe.

MISTLETOE: Jupiter, Odin, Zeus, and associated with the myths of Balder and Aeneas.

MONKSHOOD: Hecate, and associated with Cerberus.

MOONWORT: Aah, Artemis, Diana, Hina, Selene, Sin, Thoth, and all Lunar Deities.

MOSSES: Tapio.

MOTHERWORT: Various Mother Goddess figures.

MUGWORT: Artemis, Diana, and associated with the medieval legend of John the Baptist.

MULBERRY BUSH: Minerva, and associated with the classical legend of the Babylonian lovers, Pyramus and Thisbe.

MULLEIN: Circe and Ulysses.

NARCISSUS: Dis, Hades, Narcissus, Persephone, and Venus.

ORCHID: Bacchus and Orchis.

ORRIS ROOT: Aphrodite, Hera, Iris, Isis, and Osiris.

OSIERS: Hecate.

PARSLEY: Aphrodite, Persephone, Venus, and associated with death and the devil of the Christian `mythos.

PEONY: Associated with the legend of Paeon.

PENNYROYAL: Demeter.

PEPPERMINT: Zeus.

PERIWINKLE: Aphrodite.

PLANTAIN: Venus.

POPPY: Ceres, Diana, and Persephone.

PRIMROSE: Freya and Paralisos.

PURSLANE: Hermes.

RASPBERRY: Venus.

REEDS: Inanna and Pan.

ROSE: Aphrodite, Aurora, Chloris, Cupid, Demeter, Erato, Eros, Flora, Freya, Hathor, Holda, Isis, Venus, and associated with the Virgin Mary of the Christian mythos.

RUE: Mars.

RUSHES: Acis.

RYE: Ceres.

SAGE: Consus and Zeus.

SANDALWOOD: Venus.

SAXIFRAGE: Kupala.

SHAMROCK: Trefuilngid Tre-Eochair.

SOLOMON'S SEAL: Vor, and associated with the legendary King Solomon of Israel.

STRAWBERRY: Freya, Frigga, Venus, and associated with the Virgin Mary of the Christian mythos.

SUGAR CANE: Cupid, Eros, and Kama.

SUNFLOWER: Apollo and Demeter.

TANSY: Associated with the Virgin Mary and the classical legend of Ganymede.

TARRAGON: Lilith.

THISTLE: Thor, and associated with the Virgin Mary.

TI PLANT: Pele.

TREFOIL: Olwen.

VERBENA: Diana and Hermes.

VERVAIN: Aradia, Cerridwen, Demeter, Diana, Hermes, Isis, Juno, Jupiter, Mars, Mercury, Persephone, Thor, and Venus.

VIOLET: Aphrodite, Attis, Io, Venus, Zeus, and associated with the Virgin Mary.

WATER LILY: Surya and all Water Nymphs.

WOOD SORREL: All Triple Goddesses, and associated with Saint Patrick.

WORMWOOD: Artemis, Diana, the Great Mother, and all Pagan nymphs of Russia.

YARROW: The Horned God of the Wiccans, and associated with the Greek hero Achilles.

AN HERB BY ANY OTHER NAME

In days of yore, numerous herbs and plants thought to possess mystical or magickal powers were given "witchy" nicknames. Some of these old names are still used by many present-day Witches and herbalists, such as "Witch-Grass" for couch grass (*Agropyron repens*); "Witches' Bells" or "Witches' Gloves" for foxglove (*Digitalis*); "Witches' Broom" for heather (*Calluna vulgaris*); "Warlock Weed" for poison hemlock (*Conium maculatum*); "Hag-Taper" or "Witch's Candle" for mullein (*Verbascum thapsus*); "Witches' Pouches" for shepherd's purse (*Capsella bursa-pastoris*); "Gypsy Flower" for hound's-tongue (*Cynoglossam officinale*); "Gypsy Weed" for speedwell (*Veronica officinalis*); "Old Druid's Foot" for blazing star (*Chamaelirium luteum*); "Sorcerer's Violet" for periwinkle (*Vinca minor*); and "Wizard Root" for ginseng (*Panax schin-seng*).

Historically, vervain (Verbena) has been associated with witchcraft, magick, and sorcery; for this reason, it was given the appropriate nicknames of "Witchwort" and "Enchanter's Plant." In ancient Rome, it was known as the "Herb of Good Omen" and was used to decorate the altars of the gods.

Many of the herbs used by Witches have been harvested, eaten, or sacrificed in honor of certain Pagan deities. Their mythological associations are reflected in such herbal nicknames as "Jupiter's Staff" for mullein (*Verbascum thapsus*); "Jupiter's Bean" for henbane (*Hyoscyamus niger*); "Juno's Tears," "Mercury's Plant," or "Tears of Isis" for vervain (*Verbena*); and "Jupiter's Beard" or "Jupiter's Eye" for houseleek (*Sempervivum tectorum*).

In the Middle Ages, as the Christian Church gained power, the peaceful nature deities of the Old Religion were transformed into the devils of the new religion, and many of the herbs associated with Pagans became herbs of the devil and were given such nicknames as "Devil's Bit" for blazing star (*Chamaelirium luteum*); "Devil's Turnip" for bryony (*Bryonia dioica*); "Devil's Hat" for butterbur (*Petasites*); "Devil's Herb" for savin (*Juniper sabina*); "Devil's Nettle" and "Devil's Plaything" for yarrow (*Achillea millefolium*); "Devil's Vine" for hedge bindweed (*Convolvulus sepium*); "Satan's Apple" and "Devil's Candle" for European mandrake (*Mandragora officinarum*); "Devil's Bite" for hellebore (*Veratrum viride*); "Devil's Bones" for wild yam (*Dioscorea villosa*); "Devil's Apple" and "Devil's Trumpet" for jimsonweed (*Datura stramonium*); "Devil's Eye" for henbane (*Hyoscyamus niger*); "Devil's Dung" for ferula (*Ferula foetida*); "Devil's Fuge" for mistletoe (*Viscum album*); and "Devil's Root" for the peyote cactus (*Lophorora williamsii*).

In Germany and Holland, mugwort (*Artemisia vulgaris*) was known as "Saint John's Plant," for it was believed that when gathered on Saint John's Eve (Midsummer's Eve) it gave protection against sorcery, evil spirits, diseases, and misfortunes.

Tarragon (*Artemisia dracunculus*) is often called "Dragonwort" or "Little Dragon"; rue (*Ruta graveolens*) is known as the "Herb of Grace"; and basil (*Ocimum basilicum*) is the "Herb of Love."

Circles of mushrooms in grassy areas marking the periphery of underground mycelial growth are nicknamed "Fairy Rings" after the folk belief that the circles are produced by dancing fairies. Many herbs are also associated with fairy-folk and are given nicknames such as "Fairies' Horse" for ragweed (*Senecio*); "Fairy Fingers," "Fairy's Caps," "Fairy's Thimbles," and "Fairy's Glove" for foxglove (*Digitalis*); "Fairy Smoke" for Indian Pipe (*Monotropa uniflora*); "Elfwort" and "Elf Dock" for elecampane (*Inula helenium*); and "Leprechaun Clover" for shamrock or wood sorrel (*Oxalis acetosella*).

The mistletoe (*Viscum album*) was a highly revered religious and magickal herb among the ancient Druid priests of pre-Christian Britain and Gaul, and came to be known, appropriately, as "Druidswort."

Centaury (*Centaurium umbellatum*) was thought to possess great magickal powers by the Druids, who used the plant as a charm to attract good luck and repel evil. It is often called "Centaur's Hoof" and is named after the fabled centaur Chiron, who used it to heal an arrow wound.

Wormwood (*Artemisia absinthium*) was sacred to the Great Mother and is known as the "Spirit-Mother."

Lady's Mantle (*Alchemilla vulgaris*), a wild European herb, came to be known as an important magickal plant in the sixteenth century upon the discovery that overnight dew collected in the funnel-shaped folds of its semi-closed nine-lobed leaves. Alchemically minded scientists of that era regarded dew as a highly magickal substance and the plant was soon nicknamed "Alchemilla," meaning the "Little Magickal One."

The mandrake, with its mysterious human-shaped root (or *mandragora*, as it is poetically called), is a plant associated with medieval sorcery and is perhaps the most magickal of all plants and herbs. In Arabia it is called "Devil's Candle" or "Devil's Light," from the old folk belief that its leaves glow in the dark: a phenomenon caused by glowworms. The ancient Greeks called the mystical mandrake "Circe's Plant," for it was believed that the enchantress Circe used an infusion of mandrake first to enamor and then to transform her victims. The mandrake has many other nicknames, including "Man-Dragon," "Warlock Root," "Earth-Manikin," "Root of Evil," and "Little Gallows-Man."

HEALING HERBS

The following list of common physical ailments and the various herbs used throughout the ages to treat them is included here merely to give some examples of the healing power of herbs used by Witches, shamans, and folk healers. This is not intended to be a complete guide to herbal self-treatment (the methods of administration are not described here). In the event of any serious physical illness or medical emergency, you should seek professional medical care immediately.

ACNE: agrimony, burdock, chamomile, cleavers, dandelion, elder, English walnut, kidney bean, lavender, mistletoe berries, valerian, wild strawberry.

ALCOHOLISM: angelica, cannabis, cayenne, feverfew, ginger, goldenseal, mother of thyme, nerve root, passionflower, quassia, red currant, yellow jasmine.

ANEMIA: alfalfa, artichoke, barberry, blackberry, brooklime, burnet saxifrage, chives, comfrey, dandelion, elecampane, fenugreek, fumitory, gentian, ground ivy, Iceland moss, lad's love, marshmallow, milfoil, nettle, quassia, Saint John's wort, spinach, sweet flag, thyme, watercress.

ARTERIOSCLEROSIS (HARDENING OF THE AR-TERIES): arnica, artichoke, chervil, foxglove, garlic, hawthorn, mistletoe, nutmeg, olive, onion, pansy, rue, shepherd's-purse, watercress, Witch-grass.

ARTHRITIS: alder buckthorn, alfalfa, aloe, bayberry, black currant, black elder, black poplar, buckbean, burdock, buttercups, cayenne pepper, chickweed, comfrey, cramp bark, dropwort, garden violet, garlic, hops, horseradish, juniper, kava kava, life everlasting, meadow saffron, meadowsweet, monkshood, mountain holly, pokeweed, red bryony, sage, sassafras, skunk cabbage, tansy, thyme, willows, wintergreen, Witch-grass, wormwood, yew.

BRONCHIAL ASTHMA: almond, anise, arum, asefetida, balm, betony, black cohosh, bloodroot, blue vervain, boneset, burdock, California gum plant, cannabis, celandine, colic root, coltsfoot, comfrey, cubeb, daisy, dwarf nettle, elder bark, elecampane, eucalyptus, feverfew, garlic, ground ivy, heart's-ease, horehound, horseradish, hyssop, Indian tobacco, jimsonweed, lettuce, lobelia, lovage, masterwort, milkweed, mullein, myrrh, nettle, New Jersey tea, parsley, peony, prickly ash, quaking aspen, red clover, saw palmetto, skunk cabbage, speedwell, spikenard, sundew, verbena, watercress, wild black cherry, wild marjoram, yerba santa.

BRONCHITIS: angelica, anise, asafetida, barley, bearberry, betony, bilberry, black cohosh, black elder, black poplar, bloodroot, borage, buttercups, catnip, celery, chickweed, clove, clover, coltsfoot, comfrey, cowslip, cubeb, dandelion, elecampane, eucalyptus, fennel, feverfew, garden violet, garlic, goldenseal, ground ivy, heather, hemp nettle, horehound, horse chestnut, Iceland moss, Irish moss, jimsonweed, knotgrass, lad's love, lavender, licorice, lobelia, lovage, lungwort, marshmallow, mother of thyme, mountain holly, mouse-ear, mullein, New Jersey tea, onion, orris root, pansy, peach tree, plantains, pleurisy root, primrose, radish, red clover, rue, saffron, sage, Saint John's wort, sandalwood, savory, skunk cabbage, slippery elm, speedwell, spruce, sundew, sweet Cicely, sweet marjoram, verbena, watercress, yerba santa.

BRUISES: aloe, arnica, balm of Gilead, bittersweet nightshade, birch, black elder, burdock, burnet saxifrage, calendula, celery, comfrey, dwarf nettle, fenugreek, figwort, flax, garden violet, goldenrod, herb Robert, hound's-tongue, hyssop, laurel, life everlasting, lobelia, marjoram, marshmallow, mugwort, nettle, okra, olive, pennyroyal, primrose, quaking aspen, Saint John's wort, Solomon's Seal, tansy, thyme, willows, wintergreen, Witch hazel, wormwood, yerba santa.

BURNS: aloe, bittersweet nightshade, burdock, calendula, chickweed, cleavers, coltsfoot, comfrey, cucumber, gum plant, hound's-tongue, houseleek, Irish moss, lady's mantle, linseed, olive, plantain, poplars, pumpkin, quaking aspen, quince seeds, sage, Saint John's wort, slippery elm, sweet flag, willows, Witch hazel.

CANCER: barley, bloodroot, celandine, cleavers, dock, pokeweed, red clover, spurge.

CATARRH: blessed thistle, borage, goldenseal root, hound's-tongue.

CHILBLAINS: angelica, barberry, calendula, garlic, hawthorn, horseradish, lady's mantle, milfoil, mistletoe, mugwort, onion, sage, Saint Benedict's thistle, shepherd's purse, turnip, watercress.

COLDS: angelica, balm, betony, bilberry, birch, black elder, bloodroot, blue vervain, boneset, butternut, catnip, chamomile, coltsfoot, dogwood bark, life everlasting, feverfew, fig, galangal, garlic, ginger, ginseng, goldenrod (gray), ground ivy, gum plant, horehound, hyssop, Indian root, laurel, lemon, licorice, lobelia, masterwort, milfoil, pennyroyal, peppermint, pleurisy root, prickly ash, rose, safflower, sage, sarsaparilla, savory, saw palmetto, soapwort, spikenard, valerian, Virginia snakeroot, white pine, wintergreen, Witch grass, wormwood, yarrow, yerba santa.

COLIC: angelica, anise, asafetida, avens, catnip, chamomile, ginger, peppermint, rosemary, rue, unicorn root.

CONSTIPATION: agave, alder buckthorn, aloe, asparagus, basil, blue flag, boneset, bryony, buckbean, bunchberry, burdock, burning bush, butternut, calendula, castor bean, celandine, centaury, chickweed, chicory, cucumber, dandelion, dogbane, dog's mercury, elm, feverfew, fig, flax seed, fumitory, goldenseal, hedge bindweed, horehound, hyssop, larkspur, licorice, linseed oil, magnolia, mandrake, marshmallow, mugwort, mulberry, olive, pokeweed, primrose, purging flax, radish, red elder, rhubarb, rowan, sage, shepherd's purse, soapwort, sorrel, spurges, sticklewort, tamarind, wahoo, walnuts, water dock, white ash, wormwood.

COUGH: acacia, agrimony, almond, angelica, anise, asafetida, balm of Gilead, bilberry, birthroot, bitter milkwort, black cohosh, black elder, bloodroot, borage, celandine, chokecherry, coltsfoot, comfrey, corkwood, cramp bark, cubeb, dock, elecampane, English ivy, evening primrose, flax, garlic, ginseng, ground ivy, heather, horehound, horseradish, hound's-tongue, hyssop, Iceland moss, Indian root, Irish moss, jimsonweed, lad's love, lemon, lettuce, licorice, lobelia, lovage, lungwort, maidenhair fern, marshmallow, milfoil, mullein, myrrh, okra, onion, orris root, pansy, parsley, plantain, pleurisy root, quaking aspen, radish, red clover, rosemary, rue, saffron, sanicle, sarsaparilla, sassafras, skunk cabbage, slippery elm, spikenard, sundew, thyme, vervain (blue), water avens, white pine, wild black cherry, yerba santa, yew.

CRAMPS: angelica, anise, balm, belladonna, betony, black elder, blue cohosh, burnet saxifrage, buttercups, calendula, caraway, cayenne pepper, celandine, chamomile, coriander, cowslip, cramp bark, daisy, dill, fennel, garlic, henbane, lady's mantle, lavender, marjoram, masterwort, milfoil, motherwort, nerve root, peppermint, radish, rose, rosemary, rue, savory, silverweed, thyme, valerian, water mint, wild yam, wintergreen, woodruff, wormwood.

DANDRUFF: agave, chamomile, English ivy, fenugreek, figwort, marshmallow, olive, quassia, rosemary, willows.

DIABETES: artichoke, bilberry, blue cohosh, centaury, chicory, dandelion, dwarf nettle, elecampane, fenugreek, flax, goat's rue, juniper, lettuce, milfoil, nettle, onion, queen of the meadow, saw palmetto, Solomon's seal, spotted cranesbill, sumac, wild red raspberry, wintergreen.

DIARRHEA: acacia, agrimony, alum root, amaranth, apple, avens, barberry, basil, bayberry, bennet, betony, bilberry, bistort, bitter milkwort, black alder, blackberry, black cohosh, black currant, black walnut, calendula, camphor, carrot, catnip, chamomile, cinquefoil, coltsfoot, columbine, comfrey, crane's-bill, dock, dropwort, five-finger grass, garlic, ginger, goldenrod, ground ivy, herb Robert, horse chestnut, horsemint, horseweed, hound's-tongue, hyssop, Iceland moss, Judas tree, knotgrass, lady's mantle, life everlasting, loosestrife, lungwort, madder, magnolia, meadowsweet, motherwort, mullein, pansy, peppermint, periwinkle, pilewort, plantain, pomegranite rind, privet, radish, red elder, rhubarb, rowan, sage, Saint John's wort, savory, shepherd's purse, silverweed, slippery elm, sumac, tormentil, vervain, water avens, wax myrtle, white oak bark, willow bark, Witch grass, Witch hazel, woundwort.

DIPHTHERIA: lobelia.

DROPSY: blue cohosh, garlic, hawthorn, may apple.

DYSENTERY: avens, bayberry, blackberry, bloodroot, catnip, comfrey, fennel, marshmallow, Saint John's wort.

EARACHE: bay laurel, caraway, chamomile, garlic, mullein, onion, wild ginger, yarrow.

ECZEMA: aloe vera, artichoke leaves, blackberry leaves, bloodroot, broom flowers, burdock, buttercup, celandine (greater), chicory, dandelion, elecampane, heart's ease, horehound, lavender, marigold, marshmallow, mountain grape, nettle, yarrow.

EPILEPSY: blue cohosh, garlic, heart's ease, lobelia, marigold, mistletoe, mugwort, valerian.

FEMALE DISORDERS: barberry, birthroot, blue cohosh root, common groundsel, goldenseal, milfoil, pennyroyal, purple trillium, ragwort, rue, shepherd's purse, star grass, stork's-bill, tansy, yarrow.

FEVER: aconite, angelica, apple, avens, balm of Gilead, barberry, basil, birch, bird's-tongue, black currant, black elder, black poplar, blackthorn, blessed thistle, boneset, borage, buckbean, burnet saxifrage, buttercup, calendula, carline thistle, catnip, cayenne pepper, cinquefoil, cowslip, dandelion, dogbane, dogwood, dropwort, elder flowers, English ivy, English oak, eucalyptus, feverweed, fenugreek, garden violet, ginseng, goat's-rue, horehound, hyssop, Indian pipe, lad's love, lemon, life everlasting, lobelia, lovage, magnolia, mandrake, marigold, masterwort, meadowsweet, milfoil, motherwort, mountain holly, olive, passionflower, pennyroyal, pilewort, pomegranate rind, quaking aspen, quassia, raspberry, red elder, sage, sandalwood, sarsaparilla, sassafras, sticklewort, strawberry, sumac, tormentil, Virginia snakeroot, wahoo, white oak, willow bark, wintergreen, wormwood, yarrow, yerba santa.

GALL BLADDER: agrimony, artichoke, barberry, burdock, celandine, centaury, chicory, club moss, daisy, dandelion, elecampane, fumitory, garlic, gentian, hepatica, lavender, milfoil, mugwort, onion, peppermint, radish, rosemary, scarlet pimpernel, sticklewort, Witch grass, wormwood, yellow toadflax.

GALLSTONES: alder buckthorn, artichoke, barberry, chicory, dandelion, dropwort, flax, fringe tree, hyssop, mandrake, meadowsweet, milkweed, parsley, sticklewort, vervain, willows, woodruff.

GASTROENTERITIS: avens, balm, basil, bedstraw (yellow), bilberry, bistort, black currant, blue flag, broom flowers, buckbean, centaury, chamomile, cleavers, coltsfoot, elecampane, eyebright (red), five-finger grass, garlic, hyssop, knotgrass, lad's love, lady's mantle, licorice, loosestrife, marshmallow, milfoil, mullein, peppermint, plantain, sage, Saint Benedict thistle, Saint John's wort, savory, silverweed, sweet flag, thyme, water mint, wild strawberry, winter savory, Witch grass, wood sorrel.

GOUT: betony, birch, bittersweet nightshade, black mustard, buckbean, burdock, celery, chamomile, comfrey, dropwort, gentian, horseradish, jimsonweed, kava kava, meadow saffron, meadowsweet, monkshood, mountain holly, nettle, pennyroyal, quaking aspen, Saint John's wort, sarsaparilla, sassafras, speedwell, tansy, watercress, white mustard, willows, Witch grass, yerba mate.

HALITOSIS (BAD BREATH): anise, apple, bennet, caraway, cinnamon, cloves, dill, fenugreek, goldenseal, linden, lovage, myrrh, parsley, peppermint, rosemary, sage.

HEADACHE: angelica, anise, balm, basil, betony, birch, chamomile, cannabis, catnip, centaury, cleavers, dropwort, ergot, eyebright (red), fennel, feverfew, ginger, ground ivy, henna, hops, ivy, lady's mantle, lavender, lily of the valley, marshmallow, meadowsweet, mistletoe, mugwort, pennyroyal, peppermint, primrose, rose, rosemary, rue, sage, savory, shepherd's purse, speedwell, thyme, verbena, vervain, white willow, wintergreen, woodruff, wormwood, yerba santa.

HEART AILMENTS: aconite, angelica, arnica, asparagus, balm, barberry, betony, bistort, black hellebore, bloodroot, blue cohosh, borage, calendula, camphor, cayenne, cowslip, foxglove, hawthorn, lady's mantle, lemon, lily of the valley, milfoil, mistletoe, motherwort, mugwort, primrose, rosemary, rue, saffron, Saint John's wort, shepherd's purse, silverweed, valerian, wahoo, woodruff, wormseed.

HEARTBURN: chamomile, ginger, peppermint.

HEMORRHOIDS: aloe, amaranth, bayberry, birch, burdock, burnet saxifrage, chamomile, elder, goldenseal, honeysuckle, horse chestnut, horseweed, houseleek, lemon, lungwort, milfoil, nettle, onion, plantain, pilewort, pokeweed, poplar, Solomon's seal, wild black cherry, Witch hazel, yellow dock.

HEPATITIS: agrimony, dandelion, dock, greater celandine.

HERPES: bloodroot, calendula.

HIGH BLOOD PRESSURE: barberry, black cohosh, bloodroot, blue cohosh, boneset, chervil, cleavers, ergot, garden violet, garlic, ginger, hawthorn, mistletoe, onion, parsley, rue, Scotch broom, skullcap, stork's-bill, tansy, wild black cherry, yellow dock.

HOARSENESS: blackberry, black currant, chickweed, coltsfoot, comfrey, garlic, goldenseal, Iceland moss, licorice, lobelia, lungwort, maidenhair fern, marshmallow, marsh tea, mullein, okra, plantain, rowan, sage, skunk cabbage, slippery elm, wild black cherry.

INDIGESTION: angelica, anise, balm, black mustard, blessed thistle, blue gentian, buckbean, caraway, cayenne pepper, chamomile, comfrey, coriander, cornflower, cubeb, dandelion, dill, eucalyptus, fennel, feverfew, garlic, goldenseal, grindelia, hops, horsemint, hyssop, juniper, lavender, linden, lovage, magnolia, milfoil, mugwort, nutmeg, papaya, parsley, peppermint, rhubarb, rosemary, saffron, sage, salsify, sandalwood, sanicle, savory, spearmint, sweet cicely, sweet flag, valerian, wild ginger, winter savory, wormwood, yerba buena.

INFLAMMATION: arnica, borage, bryony, burnet saxifrage, chamomile, chickweed, chicory, coltsfoot, comfrey, fenugreek, ginseng, goldenseal, gumplant, hedge bindweed, hops, lobelia, monkshood, mugwort, mullein, pokeweed, sandalwood, sarsaparilla, slippery elm, Solomon's seal, tansy, willow, wintergreen, Witch hazel.

INFLUENZA: balm, birch, blackberry, blessed thistle, borage, burnet saxifrage, butternut, calendula, cinquefoil, cleavers, coltsfoot, dropwort, elder, lady's mantle, lavender, marshmallow, meadowsweet, pansy, peppermint, pleurisy root, primrose, rosemary, sage, sticklewort, yarrow.

INSOMNIA: cannabis, catnip, chamomile, cleavers, dandelion, dill, heather, hops, nerve root, passionflower, primrose, rosemary, skullcap, vervain, woodruff.

JAUNDICE: agrimony, burdock, celandine, dandelion, dock, dog's grass, parsley, Saint John's wort.

KIDNEY INFECTIONS: hawthorn, lemon, yarrow.

KIDNEY STONES: cleavers, dandelion, dog's grass, goldenrod, greater celandine, horsetail grass, parsley root.

LACTATION: angelica, anise, basil, bitter milkwort, borage, burnet saxifrage, fennel, fraxinella, goat's rue, hops, Iceland moss, lavender, parsley, wild raspberry.

LEPROSY: frankincense, garlic, myrrh.

LEUCORRHEA: balm, bearberry, bistort, black walnut, centaury, comfrey, cubeb, fenugreek, goldenseal, horehound, juniper, kava kava, lady's mantle, life everlasting, magnolia, milfoil, myrrh, plantain, ragwort, sage, Saint John's wort, slippery elm, sticklewort, sumac, tansy, tormentil, wax myrtle, wintergreen, wormwood.

MALE DISORDERS: carline thistle, club moss, melon seeds, pumpkin seeds, safflower oil, soybean oil, sunflower seeds, wheat germ.

MENOPAUSE: balm, birthwort, hawthorn, hops, lady's mantle, life root, milfoil, mistletoe, motherwort, mugwort, rosemary, rue, shepherd's purse, squaw weed, valerian, woodruff, wormwood.

MENSTRUAL PAIN: catnip, chamomile, ginger, motherwort, pennyroyal, squaw weed, sweet cicely.

MUSCLE ACHES AND PAINS: arbor vitae leaves, cayenne pepper, peppermint.

MUSCLE CRAMPS AND SPASMS: arnica, eucalyptus oil, peppermint.

NAUSEA: anise, asparagus, balm, balm of Gilead, barley, basil, blue flag, calendula, caraway, chamomile, cloves, ginger, ginseng, goldenseal, hops, horsemint, lavender, oswego tea, pennyroyal, peppermint, quaking aspen, sage, savory, spearmint, valerian, wild yam, wood betony, woodruff.

NERVOUS CONDITIONS: almond, asafetida, balm, betony, borage, catnip, celery, chamomile, hawthorn, henbane, hops, Indian pipe, jasmine, lily of the valley, motherwort, mountain laurel, nerve root, New Jersey tea, olive, pansy, passionflower, peppermint, periwinkle, queen of the meadow, rosemary, rue, sage, Saint John's wort, savory, skullcap, skunk cabbage, spruce, thyme, valerian, verbena, wild yam, Witch hazel, woodruff, wormwood.

NEURALGIA: allspice, blue cohosh, buttercup, cannabis, chamomile, cowslip, henbane, horse chestnut, hound's-tongue, kola tree, lavender, mistletoe, monkshood, mountain laurel, queen of the meadow, skullcap, Solomon's seal, valerian, wild yam, willow, woodruff, wormwood, yerba mate.

NOSEBLEED: yarrow.

OBESITY: apple, balm, centaury, chickweed, cleavers, dropwort, fennel, goldenrod, ground ivy, hops, Irish moss, meadowsweet, nettle seeds, Saint John's wort, sassafras, scurvy grass, watercress, willow.

PALSY: lavender, mistletoe.

PARALYSIS: lavender, wolfsbane.

PLEURISY: angelica, rue, sage, slippery elm, verbena.

PNEUMONIA: aconite.

POISON IVY: gum plants, impatiens pallida, jewelweed, jimsonweed, mugwort, sweet fern, yerba santa.

RASHES: hops, plantain.

RHEUMATISM: alfalfa, allspice, asparagus, birthwort, bittersweet nightshade, black birch, black cohosh, black elder, black mustard, black snakeroot, borage, boxwood, burdock, carline thistle, columbine, comfrey, coriander, cowslip, dandelion, dropwort, elderberry, feverfew, garlic, heather, henbane, horsemint, horseradish, horseweed, imperial masterwort, juniper, laurel, magnolia, meadow saffron, meadowsweet, monkshood, nettle, pansy, pipsissewa, pokeweed, poplar, quassia, rosemary, rowan, rue, sarsaparilla, sassafras, skullcap, skunk cabbage, sticklewort, sweet flag, watercress, willow, wintergreen, Witch grass, wormwood, yerba santa, yew.

SMALLPOX: catnip, marigold, saffron.

SORE THROAT: agrimony, black currant, blazing star, burdock, comfrey, ginger, horehound, lemon, lovage, mallow, myrrh, orris root, rose, sassafras, savory, slippery elm, smooth alder, smooth sumac, speedwell.

SPRAINS: comfrey, lavender, lobelia, marjoram, marigold, marshmallow, tansy, wolfsbane (arnica).

STOMACH ULCERS: alfalfa, althea, angelica, amaranth, arum, balm, balm of Gilead, bistort, burdock, calendula, chickweed, comfrey, dwarf nettle, elecampane, fenugreek, garlic, goldthread, hops, Iceland moss, knotgrass, licorice, low cudweed, marsh hibiscus, nettle, okra, pennyroyal, plantain, sage, tansy, Witch grass, wood sorrel, wormwood.

TONSILLITIS: betony, bistort, black walnut, goldenseal, lobelia, mallow, mullein, New Jersey tea, peppermint, pokeweed, rowan, sage, slippery elm, tansy, white pine, willow, witch hazel, yellow jasmine.

TOOTHACHE: angelica, balm, burnet saxifrage, chamomile, cloves, cow parsnip, grindelia, hops, lavender, mullein, myrrh, pennyroyal, periwinkle, prickly ash, rose, sassafras, savory, sweet cicely, sweet marjoram, tansy, yarrow.

TUBERCULOSIS: agave, betony, birthroot, chickweed, comfrey, cubeb, eucalyptus, fenugreek, flax, garlic, ground ivy, lungwort, milfoil, mullein, pleurisy root, sage, slippery elm, wahoo, watercress, wax myrtle, wild black cherry, yerba santa, yew.

TUMORS: Witch hazel.

TYPHOID FEVER: sage, slippery elm.

UPSET STOMACH: chamomile, gum plant, marigold, mint, peppermint, rosemary, slippery elm, sorrel, valerian, yarrow.

VARICOSE VEINS: barberry, bennet, bistort, blind nettle, burnet saxifrage, calendula, cayenne pepper, hawthorn, horse chestnut, marigold, marjoram, mistletoe, oak bark, sage, sassafras, shepherd's purse, sticklewort, tansy, wax myrtle, white oak, Witch hazel, wood sorrel.

VERTIGO: balm, betony, catnip, hawthorn, Indian pipe, lavender, lemon, mistletoe, motherwort, peppermint, rose, rue, sage, shepherd's purse.

WARTS: alder buckthorn, calendula, dandelion, fig tree, garlic, greater celandine, houseleek, lemon, mandrake, milkweed, mullein, spurge, sundew, wild sage.

WORMS: aloe, bennet, bloodroot, buckbean, carrot, catnip, cayenne pepper, cyclamen, elecampane, garlic, goat's rue, horseradish, houseleek, lad's love, larkspur, lemon, life everlasting, mugwort, mulberry, onion, papaya, pomegranate, pumpkin seeds, quassia, tamarind, tansy, tarragon, thyme, white oak, wild plum, wormseed, wormwood, woundwort.

WOUNDS: aloe vera, amaranth, arnica, betony, birthwort, bistort, blackberry, buttercup, calendula, carline thistle, cattail, chamomile, cleavers, club moss, comfrey, cowslip, cyclamen, dandelion, figwort, flax, gentian, goldenrod, goldenseal, horsemint, horse-weed, houseleek, lady's mantle, larch, lemon, linden, lungwort, mountain balm, onion, opuntia cactus, pansy, papaya, plantain, poplar, prickly ash, Saint John's wort, sanicle, slippery elm, Solomon's seal, sweet gum, sycamore maple, vervain, white pine, white pond lily, wild daisy, wild indigo, willow, Witch hazel, woundwort, yerba santa.

HERBS OF THE ZODIAC

The following is a list of herbs and their corresponding planetary rulers and astrological influences, if they have one.

ACACIA: Mars; Scorpio.
ACANTHUS: Moon.
ACONITE: Saturn; Capricorn.
ACORNS: Earth.
ADAM AND EVE ROOT: Neptune.
ADDER'S TONGUE: Moon; Cancer.
AFRICAN DAISY: Moon.
AFRICAN VIOLET: Venus.
AGARIC: Mercury and Pluto; Leo.
AGERATUM: Venus.
AGRIMONY: Jupiter; Cancer.
ALEXANDER: Jupiter; Sagittarius.
ALFALFA: Jupiter.
ALGAE: Moon; Pisces.
ALKANET: Venus.
ALL-HEAL: Mars; Scorpio.
ALLSPICE: Uranus.
ALOES: Mars and Venus.
ALSTONIA: Mercury.

AMARANTHUS: Saturn.
AMARYLLIS: Venus.
ANEMONES: Mars.
ANGELICA: Sun; Leo.
ANISE: Moon; Aquarius.
ARNICA: Saturn; Capricorn.
ARROWHEAD: Jupiter.
ARROW ROOT: Jupiter.
ARTICHOKE: Sun.
ASAFETIDA: Pluto.
ASPHODEL: Pluto.
ASPARAGUS: Jupiter.
ASPARAGUS FERN: Mars; Scorpio.
AVENS: Jupiter.
AZALEA: Mercury.
AZTEC LILY: Venus.
BALM: Jupiter; Cancer.
BALM OF GILEAD: Venus and Jupiter.
BALMONY: Neptune.
BARBERRY: Mars; Scorpio.
BARLEY: Saturn; Leo.
BASIL: Mars; Scorpio.
BAY BERRY: Mercury.
BEANS: Venus.
BEARBERRY: Mars and Pluto; Scorpio.
BEETS: Saturn.
BELLADONNA: Saturn; Capricorn.
BETONY (WATER): Jupiter; Cancer.
BETONY (WOOD): Jupiter; Aries.
BILBERRY: Jupiter.
BINDWEED: Saturn.
BIRD'S-FOOT: Saturn.
BISHOP'S WEED: Venus.
BISTORT: Saturn.
BITTERSWEET: Mercury.

BLACKBERRY: Venus; Aries.
BLADDER WRACK: Jupiter.
BLAZING STAR: Jupiter.
BLOODROOT: Venus; Scorpio.
BLUEBELL: Saturn.
BONESET: Venus and Jupiter.
BORAGE: Jupiter; Leo.
BRAMBLE: Venus; Aries and Scorpio.
BROMELIADS: Sun.
BROOKWEED: Mars.
BROOM: Mars; Scorpio.
BRYONY: Mars.
BUCKTHORN: Saturn.
BUCKWHEAT: Mercury.
BUGLEWEED: Venus.
BUGLOSS: Jupiter; Leo.
BURDOCK: Venus.
BURNET: Sun.
BUTTERBUR: Sun.
CABBAGE: Moon.
CACTI: Mars; Aries and Scorpio.
CALAMINT: Mercury.
CALLA LILY: Moon; Scorpio.
CAMPION: Saturn.
CARAWAY: Mercury.
CARDAMOM: Jupiter.
CARNATION: Jupiter.
CAROB: Saturn.
CARROTS: Mercury; Scorpio.
CASSIA: Mercury.
CATNIP: Venus.
CAYENNE: Mars; Scorpio.
CELANDINE: Sun; Leo.
CELERY: Mercury.
CENTAURY: Sun.

CHAMOMILE: Sun; Leo.
CHERVIL: Jupiter.
CHICKPEA: Venus.
CHICKWEED: Moon.
CHICORY: Jupiter and Uranus.
CHILI POWDER: Mars; Aries.
CHIVES: Mars; Scorpio.
CINNAMON: Sun.
CINQUEFOIL: Jupiter and Mercury.
CLARY SAGE: Moon.
CLEAVERS: Moon.
CLEMATIS: Saturn.
CLOVER: Venus.
CLOVES: Jupiter.
COLEWORT: Moon.
COLTSFOOT: Venus.
COLUMBINES: Venus.
COMFREY: Saturn; Capricorn.
CORIANDER: Mars; Scorpio.
CORNFLOWER: Venus and Saturn.
COSTMARY: Jupiter.
COTTON ROSE: Venus.
COTTONWEED: Venus.
COUCH GRASS: Jupiter.
COW PARSNIP: Mercury.
COWSLIP: Venus; Aries.
CRAMP BARK: Saturn.
CRANESBILL: Mars; Scorpio.
CRESS (BLACK): Mars; Scorpio.
CRESS (SCATIA): Saturn; Capricorn.
CRESS (WATER): Moon.
CROCUS: Venus.
CROSSWORT: Saturn.
CROWFOOT: Mars; Scorpio.
CUBEBS: Mars; Scorpio.

CUCKOOPINT: Mars; Scorpio.
CUCUMBER: Moon; Cancer and Scorpio.
CUDWEED: Venus.
CUMIN: Mars; Scorpio and Taurus.
CURRANTS: Jupiter.
DAFFODIL: Sun.
DAISY: Venus; Cancer.
DAMIANA: Pluto.
DANDELION: Jupiter; Sagittarius.
DARNEL: Saturn.
DEADLY NIGHTSHADE: Saturn; Capricorn.
DEAD NETTLE: Venus.
DILL: Mercury.
DITTANY: Venus.
DOCK: Jupiter.
DOG ROSE: Moon.
DOG'S GRASS: Jupiter.
DOG'S MERCURY: Mercury.
DOG-TOOTH VIOLET: Moon; Cancer
DROPWORT: Venus.
DUCKWEED: Moon; Cancer.
ELECAMPANE: Mercury and Uranus.
ENDIVE: Jupiter.
ERYNGO: Venus.
EVERLASTING: Venus.
EYEBRIGHT: Sun; Leo.
FENNEL: Mercury; Virgo.
FENUGREEK: Mercury.
FERNS: Mercury.
FEVERFEW: Venus; Sagittarius.
FIGWORT: Venus; Taurus.
FLAG: Moon.
FLAX: Mercury.
FLEABANE: Venus.
FLEAWORT: Saturn.

FLEUR-DE-LIS: Moon.

FOXGLOVE: Venus and Pluto.

FRANKINCENSE: Sun; Aquarius

FUMITORY: Saturn; Capricorn.

FURZE: Mars; Scorpio.

GALANGEL: Sun; Leo.

GARDENIA: Venus.

GARLIC: Mars; Aries and Scorpio.

GENTIAN: Mars; Scorpio.

GERANIUM: Venus; Libra.

GERMANDER: Mars and Mercury

GINGER: Moon.

GINSENG: Uranus; Scorpio.

GOAT'S RUE: Mercury; Leo.

GOLDEN ROD: Venus.

GOLDENSEAL: Venus.

GOOSEBERRY: Venus.

GOOSE GRASS: Moon.

GOUTWORT: Saturn.

GROUND IVY: Venus.

GROUNDSEL: Venus.

HARE'S EAR: Jupiter.

HARE'S FOOT: Mercury.

HEART'S EASE: Saturn.

HEATHER: Venus.

HELIOTROPE: Sun.

HELLEBORE: Saturn; Capricorn.

HEMP: Neptune and Saturn; Pisces.

HENBANE: Saturn; Capricorn.

HENNA: Jupiter.

HERB ROBERT: Venus.

HIBISCUS: Venus.

HOLLY: Saturn.

HOLLYHOCK: Venus.

HONEYSUCKLE: Mercury and Mars; Cancer.

HOPS: Mars; Aries.
HOREHOUND: Mercury.
HORSERADISH: Mars; Scorpio.
HORSETAIL: Saturn.
HOUSELEEK: Jupiter.
HYACINTH: Jupiter.
HYSSOP: Mars; Cancer.
IRIS: Moon.
IRISH MOSS: Saturn.
IVY: Saturn.
JACOB'S LADDER: Mercury.
JASMINE: Moon and Jupiter; Cancer.
JEWELWEED: Venus and Neptune.
JIMSONWEED: Saturn; Capricorn.
KAVA-KAVA: Venus.
KIDNEYWORT: Venus; Libra.
KNAPWEED: Saturn.
KNOT GRASS: Saturn.
LADIES' MANTLE: Venus.
LADY'S BEDSTRAW: Venus.
LADY'S SLIPPER: Mercury.
LADY'S SMOCK: Moon.
LAVENDER: Mercury; Virgo.
LEEKS: Mars; Scorpio.
LEMONGRASS: Venus.
LENTIL: Venus.
LETTUCE: Moon; Cancer.
LICHEN: Mars; Aries.
LICORICE: Mercury.
LILY OF THE VALLEY: Mercury and Venus.
LIVERWORT: Jupiter; Cancer.
LOBELIA: Neptune.
LOOSESTRIFE: Moon and Cancer.
LOTUS: Neptune.
LOVAGE: Sun; Taurus.

LUNGWORT: Jupiter.
LUPINE: Mars; Aries and Scorpio.
MADDER: Mars; Scorpio.
MALLOWS: Venus; Sagittarius.
MANDRAKE: Mercury.
MARIGOLD: Sun; Leo.
MARIJUANA: Saturn; Capricorn.
MARJORAM: Mercury.
MASTERWORT: Mars; Scorpio.
MAYWEED: Sun.
MEADOWSWEET: Venus and Mercury; Gemini.
MESCAL: Mars, Saturn, and Neptune.
MEZEREON: Saturn.
MILKWEED: Jupiter.
MINTS: Venus.
MISTLETOE: Sun and Jupiter.
MONEYWORT: Venus and Jupiter.
MONK'S HOOD: Saturn; Capricorn.
MOONWORT: Moon; Cancer.
MOSSES: Saturn; Capricorn and Gemini.
MOTHERWORT: Venus; Leo.
MUGWORT: Moon and Venus.
MULLEIN: Saturn.
MUSHROOMS: Earth; Taurus.
MUSTARD: Mars; Aries and Scorpio.
MYRRH: Jupiter and Saturn; Aquarius.
NARCISSUS: Neptune.
NETTLES: Mars; Aries and Scorpio.
NUTMEG: Jupiter.
OATS: Pluto; Leo and Virgo.
ONION: Mars; Aries.
OPIUM POPPY: Moon.
ORACH: Moon.
ORCHID: Venus.
OREGANO: Mars; Scorpio.

ORPINE: Moon.
ORRIS ROOT: Moon.
PANSY: Saturn; Cancer.
PARSLEY: Mercury.
PARSNIPS: Mercury.
PASSIONFLOWER: Venus and Neptune.
PATCHOULI: Pluto.
PEARL TREFOIL: Moon.
PELLITORY: Mercury.
PENNYROYAL: Venus.
PEONY: Sun; Leo.
PEPPERMINT: Venus.
PEPPERS: Mars; Aries and Scorpio.
PEPPERWORT: Mars.
PERIWINKLE: Venus.
PEYOTE: Mars and Saturn.
PILEWORT: Mars; Scorpio.
PLANTAIN: Mars and Venus.
PLEURISY ROOT: Jupiter.
PLUMBAGO: Saturn.
POISON HEMLOCK: Saturn; Capricorn.
POKEWEED: Saturn; Capricorn.
POLYPODY: Saturn.
POTATO: Saturn.
PRIMROSE: Venus; Libra.
PRIVET: Moon.
PUMPKIN: Moon.
PURSLANE: Moon.
QUEEN ANNE'S LACE: Mercury.
RADISH: Mars; Aries.
RAGWEED: Venus.
RAGWORT: Venus.
RAMPION: Venus.
RASPBERRY: Venus.
RHUBARB: Mars; Scorpio.

RICE: Sun.
ROSE (RED): Venus.
ROSE (WHITE): Moon; Libra.
ROSE HIPS: Jupiter.
ROSEMARY: Sun; Aries.
RUE: Sun; Leo.
RUSHES: Moon; Cancer.
RYE: Pluto; Virgo and Leo.
SAFFRON: Sun; Leo.
SAGE: Jupiter and Venus; Leo.
SAINT JOHN'S WORT: Sun; Leo.
SAMPHIRE: Jupiter.
SANDALWOOD: Jupiter.
SANICLE: Venus.
SARSAPARILLA: Mars and Mercury.
SASSAFRAS: Mercury.
SAVIN: Mars; Scorpio.
SAVORY: Mercury.
SAXIFRAGE: Sun.
SCABIOUS: Mercury.
SCARLET PIMPERNEL: Sun.
SCURVY GRASS: Jupiter.
SEA HOLLY: Moon; Pisces.
SEAWEED: Moon; Pisces.
SEDGE: Mercury.
SELF-HEAL: Venus.
SENNA: Mercury.
SESAME: Moon; Taurus.
SHEPHERD'S PURSE: Saturn.
SKULLCAP: Saturn.
SNAKEWEED: Saturn.
SNAPDRAGON: Mars; Scorpio.
SOAPWORT: Venus and Neptune.
SOLOMON'S SEAL: Saturn.
SOUTHERNWOOD: Mercury.

SPEEDWELL: Venus.
SPIKENARD: Mars; Scorpio and Aquarius
SPINACH: Jupiter.
SPLEENWORT: Saturn.
SPURGE: Mercury.
SQUILL: Mars; Scorpio.
STONECROP: Moon.
STRAWBERRY: Venus; Libra
SUNDEW: Sun; Cancer.
SUNFLOWER: Sun.
SWALLOWWORT: Sun.
SWEET CICELY: Jupiter.
SWEET FLAG: Moon.
TANSY: Venus; Taurus and Gemini.
TARRAGON: Mars; Scorpio.
TEA: Mercury.
TEAZLES: Venus.
THISTLE (BLESSED): Mars; Scorpio and Aries.
THISTLE (MELANCHOLY): Saturn; Capricorn.
THISTLE (OUR LADY'S): Jupiter.
THISTLE (SOW): Venus.
THISTLE (STAR): Mars; Scorpio.
THORN APPLE: Jupiter.
THYME: Venus; Aries.
TI PLANT: Jupiter.
TOADFLAX: Venus and Mars
TOBACCO: Mars; Scorpio.
TORMENTIL: Sun.
TRAILING ARBUTUS: Uranus.
TULIP: Venus.
UNICORN ROOT (FALSE): Pluto.
UNICORN ROOT (TRUE): Uranus.
VALERIAN: Mercury.
VERBENA: Venus.
VERVAIN: Venus; Taurus and Gemini.

VINES: Sun.
VIOLETS: Venus; Libra.
VIRGINIA CREEPER: Saturn.
WALLFLOWER: Moon.
WANDERING JEW: Mercury.
WATER CHESTNUT: Moon.
WATER CRESS: Moon.
WATER LILY: Moon; Cancer.
WATER MOSSES: Moon; Pisces.
WAX PLANT: Saturn.
WINTER CHERRY: Venus.
WINTERGREEN: Moon.
WISTERIA: Neptune; Aquarius.
WITCH GRASS: Jupiter.
WITCH HAZEL: Saturn.
WOAD: Saturn.
WOLFSBANE: Saturn.
WOODRUFF: Venus and Mars.
WOOD SORREL: Venus.
WORMWOOD: Mars and Pluto; Scorpio.
WOUNDWORT: Saturn.
YARROW: Venus.
YUCCA: Pluto.

8

The Witch's Kitchen

GODDESS INCENSE

(Prepare this incense when the moon is new.)

½ dram cypress oil
½ dram olive oil
½ ounce dried rose petals
½ ounce white willow bark
3 dried rowan berries
1 teaspoon anise seeds

In a small bowl, blend together the cypress and olive oils. Set aside. Using a mortar and pestle, powder and mix together the rose petals, willow bark, rowan berries, and anise seeds. Add the dry ingredients to the oil mixture and stir together well.

Consecrate the Goddess Incense with a blessing and burn it on a hot charcoal block to honor and/or invoke the Goddess. (It may also be used in healing rituals, lunar rituals, divinations, and all forms of love magick.)

To make Goddess Incense in stick or cone form, omit the cypress and olive oils, and mix a bit of gum arabic or acacia gum into the powdered herb mixture to make it sticky. Carefully dip broomstraws into it or use your fingertips to roll small bits of the mixture into cones. Allow the incense to thoroughly dry before burning.

HORNED GOD INCENSE

7 drams tincture of benzoin
½ dram sandalwood oil
½ dram frankincense oil
½ dram myrrh oil
saltpeter
1 ounce powdered charcoal
pinch of dried asafetida
pinch of dried blessed thistle
pinch of dried peppermint

In a small bowl, blend together the benzoin and all three oils. Add a small pinch of the saltpeter and stir well. Using a mortar and pestle, powder the charcoal and the dried herbs, and then slowly stir them into the oil and saltpeter mixture. Continue stirring until it forms the consistency of thick mud. Spread the mixture into a well-greased small, square glass or ceramic container (a small aluminum foil-lined plastic or metal box can also be used), and allow it to dry for at least forty-five minutes. Using a sharp knife or a white-handled athame, cut the incense into small squares, remove them from the container, and consecrate them before using.

Horned God Incense may be burned as a powerful altar incense to honor and/or invoke the Horned God (or any phallic Pagan god), banish all negative energies, and enhance the magickal works of all Wiccan rituals.

EGYPTIAN LOVE INCENSE

(Prepare this incense by the light of a pink or red candle on a night of the new moon.)

½ ounce benzoin
½ ounce cinnamon
½ ounce galangal
½ ounce frankincense
1 ounce myrrh
3 drops honey
3 drops lotus oil
1 drop rose oil
pinch of dried and powdered orris root

Using your bare hands, mix together the benzoin, cinnamon, galangal, frankincense, and myrrh in a large non-metallic bowl. Add the honey, lotus and rose oils, and orris root. Mix thoroughly as you recite the following magickal incantation:

BY THE ANCIENT AND MIGHTY POWER OF ISIS,
SUPREME GODDESS OF TEN THOUSAND
    NAMES
AND SYMBOL OF DIVINE MOTHERHOOD AND
    LOVE,
I CONSECRATE AND DEDICATE THIS INCENSE
AS A POWERFUL TOOL OF LOVE MAGICK.

BY FIRE OF THE SUN,
BY FIRE OF THE MOON,
LET THIS INCENSE BE CHARGED
IN THE DIVINE NAME OF ISIS,
THE LADY OF THE MYSTERIES
AND BEAUTIFUL GODDESS OF MAGICK
AND ENCHANTMENT.

BLESSED BE IN THE NAMES OF IAHO,
ARIAHA, ARAINAS, AND KHA.
SO MOTE IT BE!

Cover the bowl tightly with a plastic wrap and allow it to sit for at least two weeks in a dark, undisturbed place to age.

Using a mortar and pestle, grind the ingredients into a fine powder and use it in love spells as a magickal "love powder," or burn it on a hot charcoal block as a magickal incense to draw love, reunite parted lovers, or invoke ancient Egyptian deities (especially Isis and Hathor).

FRANKINCENSE

2 tablespoons powdered frankincense
1 tablespoon powdered orris root
1 teaspoon powdered clove
1 tablespoon lemon oil

Combine and mix together the frankincense, orris root and clove. Stir the lemon oil through the mixture. Put it in a clean glass jar, seal or cork tightly, and keep in a dark, cool place for two or three months before using.

Frankincense is an excellent incense to use when performing healing magick. It can also be consecrated and burned on a hot charcoal block as an altar incense to honor the Horned God and Mother Goddess.

HECATE INCENSE

½ teaspoon dried bay leaves
½ teaspoon dried mint leaves
½ teaspoon dried thyme
pinch of myrrh resin
pinch of frankincense resin
13 drops cypress oil
3 drops camphor oil

Using a mortar and pestle, crush the bay, mint, and thyme until almost powdered. Stir in the frankincense and myrrh resins. Add the cypress and camphor oils, and mix well. Store in a tightly capped jar and let the mixture age for at least two weeks before using.

Burn on a hot charcoal block during the Rite of Hecate (August 13) to honor the Goddess, or at full moon rituals as a powerful visionary incense.

INCENSE OF GOOD OMEN

5 rose petals
1½ ounces myrrh
1 ounce dragon's blood
½ ounce sassafras
½ ounce orange blossoms
½ ounce juniper
½ ounce sage
½ dram frankincense oil

Using a mortar and pestle, powder and mix all of the dry ingredients together on a night of the new moon while visualizing the things that you need or desire.

Incense of Good Omen can be burned over hot charcoals as a powerful altar incense when performing magickal spells and rituals that involve money, luck and chance.

LAMMAS RITUAL POTPOURRI

20 drops clove bud oil
25 drops sandalwood oil
1 cup oak moss
2 cups dried pink rose buds
2 cups dried red peony petals
1 cup dried amaranth flowers
1 cup dried heather flowers
½ cup dried cornflowers

Mix the clove bud and sandalwood oils with the oak moss and then add the remaining ingredients. Stir well and then store in a tightly covered ceramic or glass container.

Place in a cup or bowl on the altar at Lammas as a fragrant ritual potpourri, or cast it into an open fire or sprinkle it on hot charcoal blocks and burn as a powerful ritual incense. (Lammas Potpourri may also be put into a mojo bag and carried or worn to attract a lover.)

GODDESS OIL

½ teaspoon dried yarrow
½ teaspoon dried sweet basil
1 teaspoon powdered myrrh
3 drops rose oil
3 drops lavender oil
½ cup olive oil

Place all ingredients in a clear glass jar and gently swirl

in a clockwise direction to slowly agitate the oils. As you do this, fill your mind with images of the Goddess and visualize Her divine power as an aura of white glowing light radiating from your hands into the jar of oil, charging it with magickal energy.

Seal the jar with a tight-fitting lid and store it in a cool, dark place for at least seven days. Strain the oil through a cheesecloth and use it to anoint candles for love spells, Goddess invocations, divinations, healing rituals and all positive (white) forms of magick.

GOOD LUCK OIL

1 tablespoon dried wormwood
3 teaspoons ground nutmeg
½ teaspoon powdered mandrake root
13 drops pine oil
¼ cup olive oil

Place all ingredients in a clean glass jar and gently swirl in a clockwise direction. Seal the jar tightly and allow it to sit for thirteen nights in a cool, dark place.

Strain the oil through a cheesecloth and use it to anoint candles for wish-magick, jinx-breaking and spells to attract good luck, money and success.

HOODOO OIL

¼ cup sunflower oil
3 tablespoons honey
3 dried pumpkin seeds
6 drops honeysuckle oil
3 drops rose oil
3 drops patchouli oil

When the moon is full, crush the pumpkin seeds using

a mortar and pestle, and then mix all of the ingredients together by the light of a new white candle. Using a sterilized silver pin, prick your right thumb and add three drops of your blood to the mixture. Spit twice into the mixture and stir thrice. Store in any airtight container until you are ready to use it.

Use Hoodoo Oil to anoint candles for spellcasting, divination, spirit communication, and invocation of the Voodoo loas.

SPIRIT OIL

1 tablespoon powdered orris or serpentaria root
1 tablespoon dried Solomon's seal
1 tablespoon dried and crushed rosemary
a small pinch of powdered jade or turquoise*
3 drops sandalwood oil
3 drops mint oil
¼ cup safflower oil

*Gemstones can be easily powdered using a metal file.

Mix all of the ingredients together and store in a tightly-capped glass jar for at least three weeks in a cool, dark place.

Strain through a cheesecloth and use to anoint candles for exorcisms, seances, counterspells, purification rituals, protection against evil influences and spells to increase clairvoyant powers.

WITCHES' FLYING OINTMENT RECIPES

The notorious "Witches' Flying Ointment," a dangerous herbal concoction producing psychedelic effects, was said to be used by Witches in the Middle Ages. It consisted mainly of parsley, hemlock, water of aconite, poplar leaves, soot, bat's blood, deadly nightshade (or belladonna), henbane, and hashish.

In a large cauldron over a fire, these ingredients would be mixed together with the melted fat of an unbaptized infant, and then rubbed on various parts of the Witch's body to enable her (or him) to "fly" off to the Sabbat. (Of course Witches didn't literally fly; however, the ointment did induce incredible hallucinations, psychic visions, and astral projections.)

The following is a modern Witch's flying ointment recipe. It is safer to use and much easier to concoct:

¼ cup lard
½ teaspoon clove oil
1 teaspoon chimney soot
¼ teaspoon dried cinquefoil
¼ teaspoon dried mugwort
¼ teaspoon dried thistle
¼ teaspoon dried vervain
½ teaspoon tincture of benzoin

Using a mortar and pestle, crush the dried herbs until almost powdered. In a small cauldron or saucepan, heat the lard over a low flame until it is melted completely. Add the herbs, clove oil, and chimney soot to the lard base and mix well. Add the benzoin as a natural preservative, stir it all together clockwise, and then simmer for ten to fifteen minutes. Strain it through a cheesecloth into a small heat-resistant container, and then allow it to cool. Store it in your refrigerator or in a cool dark place until it is ready to be used.

On a night of the full moon, anoint your temples and "Third Eye" with a small amount of the flying ointment prior to astral projection or dream magick.

(PLEASE NOTE: Flying ointment is intended for external use only.)

GYPSY-WITCH LOVE POTION

1 teaspoon dried and crushed basil
1 teaspoon dried fennel
1 teaspoon dried European vervain
3 pinches ground nutmeg
¼ cup of red wine

Place all of the ingredients into a cauldron. Mix together well, and then place the cauldron over a fire. Light a pink candle which has been anointed with rose oil, and say:

CANDLE LIGHT, WARM AND BRIGHT,
IGNITE THE FLAMES OF LOVE TONIGHT.
LET MY SOUL MATE'S LOVE
BURN STRONG FOR ME.
THIS IS MY WILL, SO MOTE IT BE!

After the love potion boils for three minutes, remove the cauldron from the fire and allow it to cool. Strain the cooled liquid through a clean cheesecloth into a cup. Add a bit of honey to sweeten the potion, and then drink it.

If you desire love from a certain man or woman, concentrate upon him or her as you prepare the brew. Drink half of the potion, and then give the other half of it to your beloved to drink as soon as possible. If he or she is karmically correct for you, the spark of love will be instantly ignited. Of course, the rest is up to you.

PLEASE NOTE: The best times to prepare the Gypsy-Witch Love Potion, as with all love potions and love spells, are on Fridays (which are ruled by Venus), Saint Agnes's Eve (the night of January 20), Saint Valentine's Day (February 14), any night of the waxing moon, and whenever the moon is in the Venus-ruled signs of Taurus or Libra.

WICCAN HANDFASTING CAKE

1 cup butter
1 cup sugar
½ cup honey
5 eggs
2 cups flour
2 tablespoons grated lemon rind
2½ teaspoons lemon juice
1 teaspoon rosewater
pinch of basil
6 fresh rose geranium leaves

In a large mixing bowl, cream the butter and sugar until fluffy and light. Add the honey and mix well. Add the eggs, one at a time, beating well after each addition. Gradually add the flour and blend thoroughly with a large wooden spoon after each addition. Stir in the lemon rind, lemon juice, rose water and a pinch of basil—the herb of love. Line the bottom of a greased nine-by-five-by-three-inch loaf pan with the rose geranium leaves and then pour in the batter. Bake the cake in a preheated 350 degree oven for one hour and fifteen minutes. Remove from oven when done and let stand on a rack for twenty minutes before unmolding. Spread icing or sprinkle sugar on top of the Handfasting Cake just before serving.

OLD-FASHIONED WITCH SOAP

4 lbs. lard
13 oz. lye (1 can)
5 cups cold water

1 tablespoon lavender oil
1 tablespoon patchouli oil
1 cup fresh strawberry juice
¼ cup dried soap bark herb (optional)

In a large enamel or iron kettle, melt the lard over very low heat. (IMPORTANT NOTE: Never use aluminum pots or utensils when working with soap containing lye.) In a separate iron or enamel pot, stir together the lye and the water. Heat until small bubbles begin to appear—do not boil. Remove from the heat and slowly pour the lye solution into the lard. With a big wooden spoon, stir in the lavender and patchouli oils, the strawberry juice and soap bark herb. Simmer for about thirty minutes, stirring frequently. Pour into two-inch-deep greased enamel or glass pans and allow to cool overnight. Cut the soap into squares and leave in the pans for at least three days before removing. Place the soap bars on waxed paper and allow them to age in a draft-free area for four to six weeks before using.

9

The Magick of Trees

TREE WORSHIP

The worship of trees is the earliest form of religion. Tree worship originally involved the sacrifice of humans and animals to the "spirits of the wood" in exchange for protection against impending misfortune. Eventually, this barbarous custom was abandoned and the more civilized and less gruesome act of knocking on wood for good luck took its place and continues even today.

TREE GODS AND SPIRITS

The tree, symbolic of the phallus and sacred to various gods and goddesses, represents life and immortality.

149

Throughout history, numerous mythological associations between deities and trees have existed, such as that between Apollo and the laurel, Attis and the pine, Athena and the olive, Osiris and the cedar, and Jupiter and the mighty oak.

The tree is the most powerful and majestic symbol of vegetation, and it has played an important role in various legends of olden times. Many deities of both the ancient Greek and Roman pantheons were believed to have been born under trees, and in many myths and fables, countless heroes (as well as gods) were magickally transformed into trees as a result of either the pity or the angered wrath of the mighty gods.

Trees have been the incarnations and symbols of various deities (Gautama Buddha was incarnated as a tree spirit forty-three times), and they have also served as the abodes of spirits, nymphs, and numerous other supernatural beings to whom they were consecrated.

The jinn of ancient Arabia lived inside of trees and possessed shape-shifting powers. In Germany and Scandinavia, strange dwarf-like creatures known as "moss-wives" or "wild-women" were believed to inhabit certain trees in forests. In Russia, there were tales of one-eyed wood-demons. In South America, dangerous wood-ghosts who lured humans to their death haunted the jungles. In Japanese folklore, there were grotesque wood-spirits who possessed the head and claws of a hawk, the body of a man, and a long proboscis. In ancient Egypt and Persia, numerous gods and goddesses frequently inhabited or took on the shapes of trees (sacred sycamores in particular); and in Greece, female tree-nymphs known as dryads and hamadryads were said to live their lives linked to a particular tree, feeling any injury to bough or twig as a wound, and dying when the tree withered and died.

Just as there were mythological associations between

gods and trees, there were also associations between trees and the nymphs: Rhoea and the pomegranate, Helike and the willow, Philyra and the lime, Daphne and the laurel, and so on.

Trees are regarded with reverence throughout Africa and are believed to be inhabited by tribal gods and benevolent spirits who give sunshine and rain, make the crops grow, and bless women with fertility. However, it is a common belief among the Basoga people of Central Africa that a tree spirit will become angered if its tree is cut down and will cause the death of the tribe's chief and his entire family.

The Iroquois and other Native American tribes believed that each tree possessed its own guardian spirit or god, and it was customary to give thanks to them for their gifts of fruit.

Japanese religious texts mention Kuku-No-Chi, a god who dwells in tree trunks, and Hamori, a god who protects the leaves of trees. The Japanese also believed that each tree was protected by its own special deity.

TREES IN ANCIENT RELIGION

The tree is one of the most essential of traditional symbols, and its worship has been an important and highly influential part of the religious history of nearly every race on the face of the earth.

In the tree worship of many ancient, Pagan cultures, most trees were regarded as being female, and their sap was offered in golden goblets to the gods. All parts of the tree were believed to possess mystical powers, but saplings that grew up over the graves of sacrificed humans or animals were held especially sacred.

Trees were an essential symbol of the Chaldean religion. Sacred dendriform symbols have been found on ancient temples and engraved cylinders, and the use of tree branches in both religious and magickal ceremonies is described in sacred Chaldean texts.

In ancient Attica during the orgiastic Dionysia (the festival of the Greek wine-god Dionysus), trees were dressed up in robes and jewels to represent the god. This practice was also common at other Greek (as well as Roman) festivals.

Stylized sacred trees, surrounded by faithful followers and decorated with garlands, appear in many Indian sculptures from ancient times. (A further stage in the stylization of the sacred tree is the decorating of it with a mask or article of clothing to symbolize the deity; and lastly, the carving of the tree trunk into a statue.)

In Greece, when a god or goddess was being honored, wreaths made from the branches of his or her sacred tree would be placed upon the tree and worshipped. Various offerings and gifts, as well as the trophies of the chase and the weapons of the conquerors, would also be hung on the tree for good luck.

Even after many Pagans had been converted to the new ways of Christianity, people continued to light candles and offer small sacrifices under particular holy trees. (In modern times, Witches still hang wreaths upon certain trees and lead ring-dances under them.)

YGGDRASIL

The concept of the universe as a tree occurs repeatedly in Pagan mythology and symbolism, and is perhaps best known in its Scandinavian form where a giant evergreen ash tree known as "Yggdrasil" was believed to be the "World Tree" which binded together Heaven and the Underworld. Its mighty trunk passed through the center of the world, and its branches stretched out over the heavens and were hung with shining stars. The three goddesses of fate dwelled under its roots, along with a gigantic dragon-like serpent. Under Ygg-drasil, the Teutonic gods gathered in judgment each day.

THE TREE OF LIFE

The folklore and mythologies of many different cultures around the world contain a giant Tree of Life which is the essence of all trees, and whose fruit produces immortality when eaten by mortals.

The Tree of Life in Nahua legend was the agave—a tropical plant which was said to be discovered by the four-hundred-breasted goddess Mayauel. (According to ancient Aztec religion, the "milk" of the agave was used by the dog-headed god Xolotl to nurse the first man and woman created by the gods.)

In the Kabbalah, the Tree of Life is a mystical diagram of God, man, and the universe; and even in the Bible (Genesis, Chapter II), there is mention of a Tree of Life which grew in the Garden of Eden, along with the Tree of Knowledge of good and evil, which bore the forbidden fruit.

According to the legends of the Chinese, the Indians, and the South Americans, the souls of the dead ascend into the realm of paradise through the trunk of a sacred Tree of Life.

The apple tree was the Tree of Life worshipped by the ancient Celts. The Chinese Tree of Life was both the peach and the date palm. The Tree of Life of the Semites was also the date palm, and the Tree of Life in the Babylonian "Garden of Eden" story was the palm tree.

In India, the sacred Tree of Life ("Asvattha") was the fig tree. Like Yggdrasil, its branches reached into Heaven, while its roots descended deep into the Underworld.

The fig tree is regarded as the Tree of Life by many

peoples, and it is often worshipped as a Tree of Knowledge.

The Kayan of central Borneo believed that they were derived from the branches and leaves of a miraculous Tree of Life which, in the beginning of time, fell to earth from the heavens.

SACRED GROVES

In the Old Testament, there are a number of references to sacred groves and to the erecting of religious altars in them.

In Greek mythology, an oracle to the god Zeus was located in a sacred grove of oak trees. A sacred grove at Dodona possessed the gift of prophecy, and the vestal fires which burned in the hallowed grove at Nemi consisted of oaken sticks and logs.

A large tree within a sacred grove represented the male deity inside the Goddess as both son and lover, and the act of breaking a branch from the sacred tree was equal to the threat of the God's castration.

In the groves of Diana at Nemi, sacred kings battled any enemy who dared to break a branch from the holy trees. Patriarchal priesthoods feared the sacred groves and considered them to be evil and dangerous. Those who attempted to destroy them were punished by the curse of the Mother-Goddess, as shown in many moralizing myths such as the one in which Erysichthon is turned into a wretched, filth-eating beggar by the angry goddess Demeter.

A sacred grove of cypresses at Phlius in the Peloponnese was a haven for prison escapees, and the branches of the trees were entwined with the discarded shackles and chains from the fugitives from justice.

The seven sacred trees of the Irish grove were the

birch, willow, holly, hazel, oak, apple, and alder. Their sacred daily and planetary correspondents are:

Tree	Day	Planet
Birch	Sunday	Sun
Willow	Monday	Moon
Holly	Tuesday	Mars
Hazel	Wednesday	Mercury
Oak	Thursday	Jupiter
Apple	Friday	Venus
Alder	Saturday	Saturn

The most well-known Druid shrine was the sacred grove at Derry. It was also protected by the fear of a curse, and its magickal name is invoked to this day by the Bardic phrase "Hey Derry Down" in the chorus of ancient Celtic ballads.

TREE LAWS

In Dalmatia, the sacrifice of a chicken was required by law before any tree could be cut down; however, in many regions around the globe, cutting down a tree (or even the simple act of breaking a branch or twig) was all together illegal.

According to an old German law, the punishment for peeling off the bark of a living tree was to cut out the culprit's navel and nail it to the part of the tree which he or she had peeled. The guilty offender would then be driven round and round the tree until all of his insides were wound about its trunk to replace the stripped off bark.

In many other parts of the world, there were laws against cutting down or injuring trees, and up until the fourteenth century, even snapping off a twig was considered sinful in Lithuania.

TREES AND VAMPIRES

In the Dark Ages, juniper trees were used for protection against evil vampires in various countries around the world. Ash trees, whitethorns, and rowans were believed to possess mystical, protective qualities, and the wood from these trees in particular was carved into stakes and driven through the hearts of suspected corpses to prevent them from turning into vampires and rising out of their graves at night in search of human blood.

TREE LORE

Since ancient times, trees have been an important part of folk medicine, shamanism, divination, magick, and superstition. Their roots, bark, leaves, branches, seeds, and fruit have cured many ills; protected homes, humans, and animals against evil, bad luck, and lightning; added strength to magickal brews, potions, and aphrodisiacs; and assisted Witches and Wizards in the casting of all sorts of wondrous spells of magick.

ACACIA

In India and Patagonia, the acacia tree is believed to be inhabited by spirits, and various offerings and sacrifices are made to the tree in exchange for fertility, healing, and protection against evil and misfortune.

Acacia wood is ritually burned on the sacred altars of the Buddhists and used to prepare the sacrificial fires of the Hindus.

ALDER

In ancient times, the alder was used in idolatrous rites in honor of the goddess Astarte and in divinatory practices to diagnose diseases.

According to legend, an alder bleeds, weeps, and begins to speak when it is hewn. At one time it was against the law in Ireland to chop one down.

The alder is used in folk medicine to treat such ailments as burns, the itch, and rheumatism.

APPLE TREE

The apple tree is known in Europe as the "Tree of Immortality Through Wisdom," and its fruit has been the subject of countless proverbs and sayings.

According to Irish legends, apple trees (as well as nut trees, oak trees, and the five mystic trees representing the five senses) were believed to be produced by the trefoil (or shamrock) god Trefuilngid Tre-Eochair, who was assimilated to Saint Patrick and also known as the Triple Bearer of the Triple Key (a name which refers to the trident, or triple-phallus, designed to fertilize the Triple Goddess).

In many parts of Europe, an apple tree is planted when a baby boy is born, and it is believed that the child will grow or dwindle with the tree. The custom of planting a "Birth Tree" is also common in West Africa, Papua New Guinea, the southern United States, and parts of Dutch Borneo.

In Iroquois Indian mythology, the apple tree is the central tree of Heaven.

The wood from the apple tree is made into wands that are used to draw magick circles, and the fruit of the tree is used in love-magick, Voodoo love charms, fertility charms, divinations, and immortality spells.

Churchmen of the Middle Ages believed that sorceresses could cause demonic possession by giving poisoned or enchanted apples to their intended victims.

Bobbing for Halloween apples is a remnant of Druidic marriage divination, and it was believed in medieval Europe that a single woman could see the image of her future husband if she peeled an apple before a candle-lit mirror on Halloween night.

The apple is best known as the forbidden fruit eaten by Adam and Eve; however; the fruit of the tree was unidentified in the Bible and the apple was never actually mentioned in conjunction with the Adam and Eve story.

ASH

In Ireland, wands made of ash wood were used by the Druids in their magickal rites. In Scotland, the ash was used to protect children from sorcery; and in England, it was used as a folk remedy to cure warts.

Children were often passed through the branches of an ash tree to be cured of rupture or rickets.

Ash rods were used to magickally cure diseases in farm animals, draw magick circles, and keep serpents at bay.

BAMBOO

The bamboo tree symbolizes friendship in India, and is an emblem of the sacred fire. Its wood is commonly used in the magick rituals of the Melanesian tribes and the Semang of Malaya. In Japan, it is regarded as sacred and is connected with moon-worship and lunar magick.

BANYAN

The banyan tree is sacred to Indian seers and ascetics and is the Tree of Knowledge in Indian mythology. The Hindu god Vishnu was born under the shade of a banyan, and it was believed that anyone who dared to injure or chop one down would anger the gods and be punished by death.

BAY TREE

The bay tree is regarded as the symbol of resurrection, and is used in healing, divination, and dream-magick. The herbalists of olden times used bay roots to treat ailments of the liver, spleen, and other internal organs. They believed that the tree's berries could counteract the poison of venomous creatures and aid in treating coughs and tuberculosis. The leaves were regarded as highly mystical and were used to protect houses against lightning and thunder, and keep sorcerers and evil demons at bay.

BIRCH

In Scandinavian mythology, the birch symbolizes the rebirth of Spring.

As a tree of magick, the birch is used in purification rites and weather-working. The Witch's besom (broomstick) was traditionally made of birch.

It is an old superstition in Newfoundland that a birch broom will "sweep away the family."

A special broom made of birch twigs was used in medieval Europe as a flogging device to exorcise evil demons, imps, and ghosts.

In certain areas of Russia, it is a Whitsunday custom to
dress a birch tree in women's clothing.

CEDAR

In Mesopotamia, the cedar tree was regarded as both
deity and oracle.

The Japanese cedar (known as the "Tree of Fire") is
considered a sacred tree, and is often planted near sanc-
tuaries.

CEIBA

The five-leaved silk-cotton tree known as the ceiba pen-
tandra is the sacred tree in Santeria, and is used in six
different ways by the santeros (priests of the Santeria
religion): (1) The leaves are used in all forms of love
magick. (2) The roots are used to place offerings and to
receive the blood of animals sacrificed to a particular
god or goddess. (3) The tree trunk is used in the casting
of black magick spells. (4) The bark of the tree is used in
brews and potions for medicinal purposes. (5) The soil
around the tree is used in black magick sorcery. (6) The
shade of the tree attracts spirits and gives its supernatural power to all the spells buried beneath it.

CHERRY TREE

In fourteenth century Japan, a tree-cult existed at Ise,
and a cherry tree known as "Sakura-No-Miya" was
worshipped.

Cherries are used in love spells, aphrodisiacs, and
healing magick, while all parts of the tree are used in
folk medicine to treat such ailments as postnatal and

menstrual hemorrhage, asthma, coughs, allergies, and syphilis.

COCONUT TREE

The coconut tree was sacred in the northern regions of Italy, and its fruit was believed to make barren women fertile. The tree is used mainly in the art of divination, and in western India, its fruits and blossoms are thrown into the ocean as an offering to the gods of the sea.

CYPRESS

The cypress is the symbol of the immortal soul, death, and sorrow. Its wood was used to make the coffins of Greek heroes and the cases for Egyptian mummies. Its seeds were eaten to acquire strength, health, and youthfulness; and its fruit has been used in folk medicine to treat such ailments as bleeding gums, loose teeth, diarrhea, and dysentery.

ELDER

The elder is a small waterside tree associated with Witches and magick. In Ireland, elder sticks were said to be used by Witches as "magick horses," and in England, it is an old folk belief that a baby placed in an elderwood cradle will either pine away or be stolen by fairies. It is also said that the elder is a blessed tree and lightning can never strike it.

Burning elder sticks in a Christmas Eve fire or cutting them on Saint John's Eve is said to reveal those who practice the black arts of sorcery.

Elderberries are carried in pockets as charms to protect against poison ivy, and also worn around the neck on a necklace as a magickal remedy for dropsy.

The flowers of the elder with their sweet, heavy scent have long been associated with death and funerals, and at one time it was believed that if an elder twig planted on a grave began to grow, it was a sign that the soul of the deceased buried below was at rest.

In the old days, elder flowers were hung on stable doors to protect horses from black magick. Wreaths of elder flowers were used by the Druids to decorate sacred altars for Beltane, and to keep away evil influences.

The Native Americans called elder the "tree of music" and made magickal flutes from its branches. They also used the bark as an antidotal poultice for inflammations and painful swellings.

All parts of the elder have been used in folk medicine to treat numerous ailments and diseases.

The purplish-black berries of the elder make a delicious wine, and its dried blossoms can be used to make a relaxing tea. Elder has been used by Witches as an aphrodisiac and also as a magickal ingredient in many spells for love, protection, and prosperity.

ELM

The elm is a shade tree said to possess the mystical power to protect against lightning. It was associated with elfen folk in England, and used by the santeros of Santeria in the casting of magick spells.

According to Teutonic mythology, the first woman on Earth was created from an elm tree by the gods.

In folk medicine, the elm is used to treat swellings, coughs, skin diseases, and venereal infections.

FIG TREE

The fig tree is the symbol of peace and plenty. Its shadow is believed to be haunted by spirits, and its bark and fruit are used in both magick and folk medicine to treat various ailments and diseases.

According to the Gospels, the fig tree was "cursed with barrenness" by Jesus Christ because it refused to produce fruit for him out of its season (Mark II: 13–22). The Book of Genesis states that the leaves of the fig tree were used by Adam and Eve, as soon as they acquired knowledge, to cover their nakedness.

HAZEL

The hazel tree has always been associated with Witches, and the very name "witch-hazel" remains today. The tree has also been associated with the god Thor.

Hazel is known as the "Tree of Wisdom" (especially in Irish legend), and it is used in magickal spells for immortality, protection, and healing. Hazel rods were believed to possess divinatory properties, and have long been used by dowsers to locate buried treasure and underground water. Hazel rods have also been traditionally used as wands by white magicians, and to protect animals against bewitchment by fairies or impious demons. According to Welsh folklore, hazel twigs woven into a "wishing cap" can be used to make wishes come true.

LAUREL

The laurel tree is the symbol of immortality, victory, and peace. It is said to be able to endow prophets with visions, and was associated with poetic inspiration.

The leaves of the laurel tree were chewed by female devotees of the Triple Goddess at Tempe to induce a poetic and erotic frenzy. They were also chewed by the Pythian priestess of the Delphic oracle for oracular inspiration.

The laurel is widely used in all forms of love-magick, wish-magick, and healing.

LIME TREE

In Germany, the lime tree was held sacred. According to folk legends and superstitions, it was haunted by dwarfs and possessed the power to make heroes fall into an enchanted sleep.

The fruit of the lime tree is used mainly in love-magick; however, in certain parts of India, it is the main ingredient in many powerful curses.

In folk medicine, the lime is used as a plaster for wounds, and to treat colds, sore throat, and scurvy.

MAPLE

The maple tree is the symbol of reserve. At one time, its branches were commonly used as divining rods to locate underground water. Its leaves are celebrated by the Japanese in blossom festivals, and a decoction made from its bark is used by various North American Indian tribes to induce vomiting.

MYRTLE

The myrtle is an evergreen tree associated symbolically with love and marriage, and sacred to many love goddesses. It also was the symbol of authority, immortality, death, and resurrection.

Wreaths of myrtle blossoms were worn by ancient Roman brides on their wedding day; however, myrtle also was the symbol of unlawful or incestuous love, and it was often banned from many religious ceremonies. In folk magick, myrtle is used in love spells, charms, passion aphrodisiacs, and spells to attract good fortune.

OAK

The oak is a tree with many ancient mythological and magickal associations. In the Alexandrian tradition of Wicca, the oak symbolizes the waxing year aspects of the Horned God. It was regarded as an "oracle tree" by the Greek philosopher Socrates, and as the most sacred of trees by the ancient Celtic Druids, who believed that the leaves possessed great supernatural powers to heal and renew strength. Acorns (the "fruit" of the oak tree) were eaten by the Druids in preparation for prophesying.

The ancient Romans also believed in the wondrous power of the oak tree, and to protect themselves against forces of evil, they wore wreaths made from oak leaves on their heads as protective crowns.

Human sacrifices were made to the Phoenician god Baal "under every leafy oak" (Ezekial 6:13), and in Estonia, the blood of slaughtered animals was poured on oak roots as a libation to the gods.

The oak is the traditional and essential wood used for Yule logs and Midsummer Night bonfires. Oak branches are used in Wiccan spells to attract good luck, and the bark from the tree is made into magickal incenses to honor the gods and goddesses to whom the oak tree is sacred. And in folk medicine, oak tea has been used to treat such ailments as pinworms, gallstones, loose teeth, and venereal disease.

OLIVE TREE

The olive tree is the symbol of peace and divine blessings. Its branches were made into crowns and worn by Greek brides, Roman conquerors, and the gods who lived atop Mount Olympus. Olive branches were also placed on chimneys and over doors to ward off lightning and keep sorcerers, demons, and wicked ghosts at bay.

The olive tree and its fruit have been used in healing spells, love-magick, and ancient fertility rites. Its oil has been used to anoint altar candles, bless religious statues, and fuel sacred temple lamps.

ORANGE TREE

The orange tree is the symbol of eternal love, chastity, and purity. Its blossoms were worn as bridal flowers, and its fruit was used by Voodoo practitioners in love-magick, and by European sorcerers in sympathetic black magick.

PALM

The palm is the Tree of Life and the dwelling place of the Goddess in many ancient myths. It is used in fertility rituals and Santeria weather-working magick.

PEACH TREE

In China, the peach is an emblem of longevity and a sacred symbol of the Goddess's yoni. The tree was believed to possess strong spiritual forces, and magick wands made from its twigs were used by Chinese wizards in immortality spells, fertility rites, and rituals to keep demons and evil spirits at bay.

The peach tree symbolizes fertility in Japan, and its wood is used there as divining rods by water-witches. Peach sticks are used in folk medicine to treat upset stomach, swollen abdomen, and pains of the heart. According to an old folk belief in Italy and the southern regions of the United States, warts can be cured by burying peach leaves.

PEAR TREE

In many parts of Europe, a pear tree is planted when a baby girl is born, and it is believed that the child will grow or dwindle with the tree.

PINE

The pine tree symbolizes life, longevity, and immortality. The pine cone is the Semitic symbol of life.

In Japanese mythology, the spirits of the pine tree are known as Jo and Uba. Pine trees are the symbol of fidelity in marriage, and there are numerous myths about devoted lovers being magickally transformed into pine trees.

The boughs of the pine are used in many Native American ceremonies, and its pitch smoke is used by the Indians to treat such ailments as rheumatism, coughs, and colds.

Pines are planted as "marriage trees" in the Tyrol, and used by Witches in Europe and the United States for protection, healing, and spells to attract the affections of another. Pine incense is commonly used in counter-magick and purification rites.

POPLAR

The white poplar is regarded as a tree of the Autumn Equinox and of old age. In pre-Hellenic Greece, the black poplar was used as a "funeral tree" and was sacred to Mother Earth.

In ancient Roman folklore, poplar trees were sacred to the hero Hercules, and in seventeenth century England, its leaves were accounted an important ingredient in "hell-broths" and magickal charms.

ROWAN

The rowan tree (also known as the mountain ash) is a tree with many mythic and magickal associations. It was a sacred tree of the Druids, and was believed to be a protection against sorcery and evil spirits in the Middle Ages.

The berries of the rowan were used to heal the wounds of those injured in battle and were believed to give a man an extra year of life. In modern times, the dried berries are ground and made into magickal incenses which are burned to ritually invoke the Goddess, spirit guides, Witches' familiars, or elemental spirits.

Rowan leaves are used in love divinations and spells or rituals designed to enhance one's poetic creativity.

In days of yore, rowan tree Witch Day was celebrated at the old Celtic festival of Beltane (May Day) which is now one of the four major Sabbats celebrated by Witches.

WILLOW

The willow, a tree often found growing near sacred wells, has long been associated with Witchcraft and Goddess-worship. It was regarded sacred by Witches and Pagan poets for all parts of it are usable in the practice of magick. The wood makes excellent wands for healing rituals and moon-magick, and can also be used in talismans when one seeks the protection of the Goddess.

Pussy willows, which are associated with both healing and springtime, are appropriate altar decorations for Candlemas, as this Sabbat (also known as Imbolc) is the festival of Brigid—the Pagan goddess of healing and of sacred wells. Pussy willows were used by the Druids as protective charms, and in the Middle Ages, it was a common belief that the familiars of Witches grew from pussy willows.

In northern Europe, the willow tree was so strongly connected with the Old Religion that even the word "Witch" is derived from the same ancient word for willow.

In China, the willow is regarded as the Tree of Immortality; and in Europe, it is the symbol of eloquence.

YEW

The yew, like other conifers, is known as a "Tree of Immortality" in many parts of the world. It was commonly used in the practice of medieval sorcery, and was one of Witch-Goddess Hecate's mystical cauldron ingredients in Shakespeare's *Macbeth* (Act IV: Scene 1).

According to old folk superstition, a man or woman who dares to sleep in the shade of a yew tree is sure to either die a horrible death or fall into an enchanted sleep.

PLANETARY AND ZODIACAL CORRESPONDENCES

The following is a list of trees and their corresponding planetary rulers and astrological influences, if they have one.

ALDER: Venus; Cancer (Black Alder) and Pisces (Common Alder).
ALMOND: Sun.
APPLE TREE: Venus; Libra and Taurus.
APRICOT TREE: Venus and Neptune.
ASH: Sun.
ASPEN: Mercury.
AVOCADO: Venus.
BALSAM: Mercury.
BANANA TREE: Moon; Scorpio.
BANYAN: Jupiter.
BAY: Sun; Leo.
BAYBERRY: Mercury.
BAY LAUREL: See *BAY.*
BEECH: Saturn; Sagittarius.
BERGAMOT: Venus.
BIRCH: Venus.
BO TREE: Jupiter.
BOX: Saturn.
BREADFRUIT TREE: Venus.
CASHEW TREE: Mars; Scorpio.
CEDAR: Mercury.
CHERRY TREE: Venus; Libra.
CHESTNUT: Jupiter.
COCONUT TREE: Venus.
COFFEE TREE: Mercury and Uranus.
CYPRESS: Saturn; Capricorn.
DOGWOOD: Venus and Neptune.
ELDER: Venus.
ELM: Saturn; Sagittarius.
EUCALYPTUS: Pluto.
FIG TREE: Jupiter.
FIR: Jupiter.
HAWTHORN: Mars.
HAZEL: Mercury.

HEMLOCK: Saturn; Capricorn.
HOLLY OAK: See *ILEX.*
HOLM OAK: See *ILEX.*
ILEX: Saturn; Capricorn.
JUNIPER: Sun and Mars
KOLA: Uranus.
LAUREL: Sun; Leo.
LIME TREE: Jupiter.
MAGNOLIA: Jupiter.
MANGO TREE: Moon.
MAPLE: Jupiter.
MASTIC: Mars; Scorpio.
MEDLAR: Saturn.
MOUNTAIN ASH: Moon.
MULBERRY TREE: Mercury and Jupiter
MYRRH: Jupiter; Aquarius.
MYRTLE: Venus.
NUTMEG: Jupiter and Uranus.
OAK: Jupiter; Sagittarius.
OLIVE TREE: Sun and Jupiter.
ORANGE TREE: Venus and Neptune; Leo.
PALM: Sun; Scorpio.
PEACH TREE: Venus and Neptune.
PEAR TREE: Venus and Neptune.
PEEPUL: Jupiter.
PINE: Saturn.
PIPAL: See *PEEPUL.*
PLANE-TREE: Venus and Jupiter.
PLUM TREE: Venus.
POMEGRANATE: Venus, Mercury, and Uranus.
POPLAR: Saturn.
QUINCE: Saturn.
ROWAN: Moon.
SERVICE-TREE: Saturn.
STORAX: Sun.

SUMAC: Jupiter.
SYCAMORE: Venus and Jupiter.
TAMARIND: Saturn.
WALNUT: Sun.
WILLOW: Moon.
YEW: Saturn; Capricorn.

TREES OF THE PAGAN DEITIES, NYMPHS, AND HEROES

The following trees are sacred to the Pagan deities, nymphs and heroes listed after them.

ALDER: Bran.
ALMOND: Artemis, Attis, Chandra, Hecate, Jupiter, Phyllis, and Zeus.
APPLE TREE: Aphrodite, Flora, Hercules, the Hesperides, Frey, Idhunn, Pomona, and all Love Goddesses.
APRICOT TREE: Venus.
ASH: Akka, Mars, Odin, Poseidon, and Rauni.
ASPEN: Gaia (Mother Earth), the Maruts, Nunu, and Zeus.
AVOCADO: Flora and Pomona.
BANANA TREE: Kanaloa.
BANYAN: Hina, Shu, Siva, Vishnu, and Zeus.
BAY LAUREL: Apollo, Adonis, Buddha, Ra, Artemis, Gaia (Mother Earth), Mars, Helios, Aesculapius, and Daphne.
BEECH: Bacchus, Diana, Dionysus, and Hercules.
BIRCH: Thor, Kupala, and the Lady of the Woods.
BO TREE: Buddha.
BREADFRUIT TREE: Pukuha Kana and Opimea.
CEDAR: Artemis, Ea, and Wotan.
CHERRY TREE: Flora, Pomona, and Maya, the Virgin Mother of Buddha.

COCONUT TREE: Ganymede and Tamaa.
CYPRESS: Ahura Mazda, Apollo, Artemis, Astarte, Beroth, Cupid, Dis, the Fates, the Furies, Hades, Hercules, Jove, Melcarth, Mithra, Ohrmazd, Pluto, Saturn, and Zoroaster.
DOGWOOD: Apollo, Consus, and Mars.
ELDER: the Dryads, Elle Woman, Freya, Holda, Hylde-Moer, Venus, and all Mother Goddess figures.
ELM: the Devas, Embla, Ut, and Vertumnus.
FICUS: Romulus and Remus.
FIG: Bacchus, Brahma, Dionysus, Flora, Jesus Christ, Juno Caprotina, Mars, Mohammed, Pluto, Pomona, Zeus, and the Indo-Iranian Great Mother.
FIR: Bacchus, Dionysus, Tapio, Byblos, Athene, Pan, Cybele, Artemis, Diana, and other Lunar Goddesses.
HAWTHORN: Cardea and Hymen.
HAZEL: Thor and Chandra.
ILEX: Faunus.
MANGO TREE: Pattini.
MAPLE: Nanabozho.
MULBERRY: Flora, Minerva, Pomona, and San Ku Fu Jen.
MYRRH: Adonis, Aphrodite, Cybele, Demeter, Hecate, Juno, Mara, Myrrha, Ra, Rhea, and Saturn.
MYRTLE: Alcina, Aphrodite, Artemis, Astarte, Dionysus, Hathor, Myrsine, Myrtelus, and Venus.
OAK: Allah, Ares, Balder, Blodeuwedd, Brahma, Ceres, Dagda, Demeter, Diana, Dianus, the Dryads, Hades, Har Hou, Hera, Hercules, Horus, Janicot, Jehova, Jumala, Jupiter, Kashiwa-No-Kami, Mars, Odin, Perkunas, Perun, Pluto, Taara, Thor, Zeus, and all Thunder Gods.
OLIVE TREE: Amen-Ra, Apollo, Aristaeus, Athena, Brahma, Flora, Ganymede, Indra, Jupiter, Minerva, Pomona, Poseidon, Wotan, Zeus, and all Sun Gods.
ORANGE TREE: Hera and Zeus.

PALM: Aphrodite, Apollo, Astarte, Baal·Peor, Chango, Hanuman, Hermes, Mercury, and Sarasvati.

PEACH TREE: Flora, Pomona, Shou-Hsing, and Wang Mu.

PEAR TREE: Flora, Hera, and Pomona.

PINE: Attis, Cybele, Dionysus, Pan, Poseidon, Rhea, Shou-Hsing, and Silvanus.

PLANE TREE: Helen.

PLUM TREE: Flora and Pomona.

POMEGRANATE: Du'uzu, Hera, Kubaba, Mercury, Persephone, Saturn, and Uranus.

POPLAR: Brahma, Dis, the Heliades, Hercules, Persephone, Phaeton, Pluto, and Zeus.

QUINCE: Aphrodite and Venus.

ROWAN: all Moon Goddesses.

STORAX: Loki, Mercury, and Thoth.

SYCAMORE: all Egyptian Gods and Goddesses.

TAMARISK: Apollo.

WALNUT: Dionysus.

WILLOW: Artemis, Beli, Brigid, Circe, Hecate, Helice, Hera, Hermes, Orpheus, Osiris, Persephone, and all death aspects of the Triple Moon Goddess.

YEW: Hecate and Saturn.

OAK SPELL FOR GOOD HEALTH

For good health throughout the year, according to an old Welsh custom, rub the palm of your left hand on an oak tree in silence on Saint John's Day.

ACORN LOVE DIVINATION

Place two acorns in a bucket filled with fresh rain water. If they float toward each other and touch, it indicates true love and marriage; if they float away from each other, there will be no wedding in the near future.

MYRTLE SPELL FOR LOVE AND PEACE

To bring love and peace to your home, plant a myrtle tree on each side of your front door when the moon is in either the sign of Taurus or the sign of Libra.

HOUSE BLESSING

To bless a house and exorcise all negative energies from it, hang bay laurel in the home, burn elder blossoms or pine incense, or place rowan leaves in each room on a night when the moon is full.

GOOD LUCK SPELL

On a night when the moon is in a waxing phase, burn dried juniper needles on a hot charcoal as a powerful magickal incense to attract good luck. An amulet made of dried juniper berries can also be worn or carried for good luck.

10

Dream Magick

Dream Magick is as old as mankind and has always played an important role in the Wicca Craft. Dreams are regarded as the most reliable of omens, and since early times, Witches, Pagan priests and priestesses, and Shamans have used them to divine the future. (The technical term used for the art and practice of divination by dreams is "oneiromancy.")

There are many different types of dreams: nightmares or distorted imagery which are often caused by environmental pressures or physical ailment; dreams which are caused by suppressed emotions; out-of-body experiences (also known as Astral Projections); and prophetic dreams which are vivid dreams pertaining to future events that come true.

A significant number of dreams are prophetic in nature, especially those which occur three nights in a row, according to folk superstition. Prophetic dreams, when correctly interpretated, can reveal the future either through direct pictures or by symbolism.

When sacred or transcendental images appear in a dream, it is called a high dream.

Telepathic dreams (also known as ESP dreams) are experiences in which the dreamer picks up thought energies from another person or a spirit. (Dreams of this nature generally pertain to events of the present.)

Psychic dreams are dreams which contain important messages, warnings, and other communications. This particular type of dream is often so strong and profound that it awakens the dreamer from his or her sleep.

Lucid dreaming is a term which is applied when a sleeping person who is in the dream state is consciously aware that he or she is dreaming.

Dreams are highly symbolic, and it is important to record them in a dream book or diary when you first wake up so that you will not forget them later. (According to certain folk superstitions, however, it is considered *lucky* for one to forget a dream from the previous night.) After recording your dreams (and nightmares), you can then look for recurring patterns and symbols, and interpret them using a dream dictionary.

There are numerous dream dictionaries and dream analysis books on the market today. They are available at nearly every bookstore and library. Some dream books contain dream symbol interpretations, some contain superstitions and old folk beliefs, and some contain a combination of the two.

One of the oldest formal writings on dream interpretation is *A Treatise of the Interpretation of Sundry Dreams*, which was originally published in the early seventeenth century. However, the oldest published dictionary of dreams and their occult significance is most likely the four-volume opus of dream interpretation written in the year 150 A.D. by the Greek soothsayer Artemidorus.

Many dreams of a prophetic nature can be deliberately induced by means of meditation, magickal spells, rituals, and even herbal brews.

To dream about the future, according to an old folk belief in Wales, a person must gather a mistletoe sprig on Saint John's Eve and place it under his or her pillow at night before going to bed.

To experience prophetic dreams, pick a red rose during the early morning hours of Midsummer's Day, and fumigate it for five minutes over a brazier of burning sulfur and brimstone. On a piece of parchment, write your name and the name of your lover. Wrap the rose in the parchment, seal it thrice with wax, and then bury it in the same spot where the rose was picked. On midnight of the sixth day of the seventh month, dig up the rose and sleep with it under your pillow for three nights in a row.

According to an old book of folk magick and divination, to see your future spouse in a dream, stick nine pins into the blade bone of a hare and place it under your pillow on a night when the moon is full.

To receive a dream of your future husband or wife, place two laurel leaves under your pillow on Saint Valentine's Day before you go to bed.

On a night of the full moon, place under your pillow the tarot card known as "The Lovers" to induce prophetic dreams about your future lover.

To make bachelors see their future brides in a dream, according to a medieval treatise on dream divination, mix together magnate dust and powdered coral with the blood of a white pigeon to form a dough. Enclose it in a large fig, wrap it in a piece of blue cloth, and then wear it around your neck when you go to sleep.

To dream of your future husband, sleep with a petticoat, garter, daisy roots, an onion, or a piece of wedding cake under your head. Tie a poplar branch to your stockings or socks and place them under your pillow, or rub your temples with a few drops of dove's blood before going to sleep.

To dream of your future marriage mate, according to an old Irish method of dream divination, gather ten ivy leaves in silence on Samhain night. Throw away one of the leaves and place the remaining ones under your pillow before going to bed.

To dream of your future spouse, collect nine leaves of a "female" holly at the stroke of midnight on a Friday (the day of the week ruled by Venus). Place the leaves in a three-cornered handkerchief tied with nine knots, and place the charm under your pillow before going to sleep. (PLEASE NOTE: This charm will not work if you speak any words before the following sunrise.)

Pluck some wild yarrow from a graveyard, and place it under your pillow at night before going to sleep. Your lover will appear before you in a dream.

YARROW LOVE VISION SPELL

To receive a psychic dream vision of your future lover, sew an ounce of yarrow herb into a small square of red flannel, and place it under your pillow at night before going to bed. Close your eyes and recite these magickal words:

"THOU HERBE OF VENUS TREE
THY TRUE NAME IS YARROW.

NOW WHO MY TRUE LOVE MUST BE
PRAY TELL THOU ME TOMORROW."

PROPHETIC DREAM SPELL

To conjure forth a prophetic dream, perform this spell
on a night when the moon is full and in the sign of
Scorpio or Aquarius. (For best results, it is advisable to
fast with water for one whole day before performing
this spell.)

Into a cauldron (or large kettle) of boiling water,
throw a pinch each of white sand, powdered cat's-eye
(gemstone), and some old chimney soot. Using a mortar
and pestle, grind and mix together a small quantity of
St. John's wort, frankincense, adder's tongue, and mandrake root. Add three tablespoons of the ground herbal
mixture to the cauldron water, and stir it thoroughly
with a large wooden spoon as you recite the following
magickal rhyme:

ST. JOHN'S WORT GATHERED BY NIGHT
FRANKINCENSE AND SAND OF WHITE
ADDER'S TONGUE AND MANDRAKE ROOT
CAT'S EYE POWDERED AND CHIMNEY SOOT
I MIX TOGETHER IN THIS CAULDRON OF STEAM
TO CONJURE FORTH A PROPHETIC DREAM

Let the magickal mixture bubble for a while, and then
remove the cauldron from the fire.

After it has cooled, draw a bath and add a few drops
of the brew to the bathwater. Light a purple candle and
place it near the tub. Remove your clothes and soak
your body in the relaxing herbal bath as you gaze into
the flame of the candle. Open your heart and mind to
the Goddess and chant Her name either out loud or

telephatically until you feel Her divine presence enter you.

After bathing, wrap your body in a white or purple robe, sprinkle a bit of the brew in a circle around your bed, and say:

> I CONSECRATE THIS DREAM CIRCLE
> IN THE NAME OF THE GODDESS.
> BLESSED BE!

Now sprinkle a bit of the brew upon your pillow, and then lay yourself down to sleep. Before the rising of the sun, you will experience one or more prophetic dreams.

HERBS OF DREAM MAGICK

The following herbs are traditionally used by Witches in magickal dream pillows and potions to induce prophetic dream visions:

adder's tongue	marigold
agrimony	mistletoe
anise	mugwort
camphor	onion
celandine (lesser)	peppermint
cinnamon	purslane
daisy	rose
holly	Saint John's wort
hops	verbena
ivy	vervain
lemon verbena	wormwood
mandrake root	yarrow

11

Pagan Periodicals

This is an up-to-date alphabetical list of various newsletters and journals that are published throughout the United States by and/or of interest to Pagans and Wiccans.

Many of these publications contain important Wiccan news, spells, Sabbat ritual outlines, information about herbs, book reviews, and Pagan contacts.

When writing to any of the following periodicals to order sample copies, please let them know that you saw their listing in this book. (IMPORTANT: When writing to any journal or newsletter to request additional information or to submit material for publication, *always* be sure to include a self-addressed stamped envelope with adequate return postage.)

THE ANCIENT ARTS
Sample copy: $4.00
The Ancient Arts
P.O. Box 3127
Morgantown, WV 26505

ASYNJUR
A journal of the Northern Goddesses
Sample copy: $3.00
Asynjur
P.O. Box 567
Granville, OH 43023

BEING
A celebration of Spirit, Mind and Body
Sample subjects: spirit/god/goddess related, fantasy/
    sword/sorcerer/ess, etc.
Sample copy: $3.00
Being
P.O. Box 417
Oceanside, CA 92054

BELLADONNA
Sample copy: $4.00
Belladonna
P.O. Box 935
Simpsonville, SC 29681

THE CINCINNATI JOURNAL OF MAGICK
Sample copy: $6.00
Black Moon Publishing
P.O. Box 19469
Cincinnati, OH 45219-0469

COMPOST NEWSLETTER
"A magazine of humor, satire, and bad taste, both in
the Craft and out."
Sample copy: $2.00 (please make checks and money
orders payable to: V. Walker for CNL)
Compost Newsletter
729 5th Avenue
San Francisco
CA 94118

CONVERGING PATHS
A Pagan journal which "focuses on Traditional ways
of Wicca, its roots and current directions.
Published four times a year."
Sample copy: $4.00 (U.S./Canada); $6.00 for overseas
(U.S. funds or I.M.O. only)
Converging Paths
P.O. Box 63
Mt. Horeb, WI 53572

DHARMA COMBAT
"An unedited reader-written forum about religion,
metaphysics and spirituality."
Sample copy: $2.00
Dharma Combat
P.O. Box 20593
Sun Valley, NV 89433

FIREHEART
"A journal of Magick and Spiritual Transformation.
Fireheart is published by the EarthSpirit
Community, a national network of Pagans and
other Earth-centered people." Sample copy: $4.00
FireHeart
P.O. Box 462
Maynard, MA 01754

GEORGIAN NEWSLETTER
Sample copy: $1.00 "and patience"
The Georgian Newsletter
1980 Verde
Bakersfield, CA 93304

GOLDEN ISIS MAGAZINE
Salem's Neo-Pagan quarterly journal of magick,
Goddess-inspired poetry, astrology, Wiccan news,
mystical Pagan art, reviews, letters, ads, contacts,
and much more.
Free writer's guidelines and occult catalogue for
SASE. Sample copy: $3.00; one year subscription:
$10.00
Golden Isis Magazine
G. Dunwich, Editor
7131 Owensmouth, Suite # C-66
Canoga Park, CA 91303

THE GREEN EGG
"The 1970's foremost magazine of Neo-Paganism has
returned to deliver an interdisciplinary treasure
trove: Shamanism, Goddess lore, psychic
development, Gaea and environmental activism,
suppressed history, alternative sexuality, plus an
uncensored Readers Forum."
Sample copy: $5.00
The Green Egg
P.O. Box 1542
Ukiah, CA 95482

HALLOWS
"The quarterly journal of the Grail Quest Wicca.
Controversial articles, the(a)ological speculation,

and literary reviews for Pagans not afraid to be
challenged."
Free sample copy
Hallows
c/o Keepers of the Cauldron
P.O. Box 1108
Glen Allen, VA 23060

K.A.M
"A journal of Traditional Wicca."
Sample copy: $3.00
K.A.M.
P.O. Box 2513
Kensington, MD 20891

KELTRIA
"A journal of Druidism and Keltic Magick. This
  quarterly journal promotes Druidic education and
  fellowship through articles of theology, herbology,
  ritual, art, music, and philosophy."
Sample copy: $2.00
Keltria
P.O. Box 33284
Minneapolis, MN 55433

LLEWELLYN NEW TIMES
A magazine/catalogue of Astrology, Magick, Occult,
  Nature Spirituality and New Age books, tapes and
  services. Reviews, articles, sales, events, calendar,
  answer column, ads.
Sample copy $2.00
Llewellyn New Times
P.O. Box 64383
St. Paul, MN 55164

THE MAGICAL CONFLUENCE
Sample copy: $3.00
The Magical Confluence
P.O. Box 230111
St. Louis, MO 63123

THE MAGIC WAND
"A journal for serious, practicing Pagans. Magick,
Stone Craft, Herbalism, Herstory, Solitary Craft,
and much more!"
Sample copy: $2.00 (eight issues for $8.00)
Magic Wand
P.O. Box 27164
Detroit, MI 48227

NORTHWIND NETWORK
"A Pagan paper focusing on Goddess information,
rituals and networking. Reader participation
encouraged."
Sample copy: $1.50
North Wind Network
Box 14902
Columbus, OH 43214

OF A LIKE MIND
"A women's spiritual newspaper and network
dedicated to bringing together women following
positive paths to spiritual growth. Its focus is on
women's spirituality, Goddess religions, Paganism,
and our Earth connections from a feminist
perspective."
Sample copy: $3.00
Of a Like Mind
Box 6021
Madison, WI 53716

PACIFIC CIRCLE NEWSLETTER
Free sample copy
Pacific Circle Newsletter
P.O. Box 9513
North Hollywood, CA 91609

PAGAN FREE PRESS NEWSLETTER
An "open forum of positive, practical Neo-Paganism,
    Wicca, Shamanism, and Folk Ways."
Sample copy: $1.00
P.F.P.
P.O. Box 55223
Tulsa, OK 74155

PAGAN NUUS
The Newsletter of the Covenant of Unitarian
    Universalist Pagans. Articles, book and movie
    reviews, graphics, poetry, etc.
Sample copy: $1.00–$2.00 ("sliding scale")
Pagan Nuus
P.O. Box 640
Cambridge, MA 02140

PALLAS SOCIETY NEWS
"Quarterly Southern California based Craft/Pagan
    magazine featuring articles on different paths,
    herbs, reviews, rituals, national and Southern
    California Pagan/Craft news, and much more.
    Reader in-put encouraged."
Sample copy: $3.00
Pallas Society News
P.O. Box 18211
Encino, CA 91316

PANEGYRIA
"A Journal of the Aquarian Tabernacle Church.
Published eight times a year on the major
holidays. News of interest to Pagans in the Pacific
Northwest and beyond.
Send three 25¢ postage stamps for free sample copy.
Panegyria
P.O. Box 85507 (Dept. GI)
Seattle, WA 98145
Telephone: (206) 527-2426 (recorded message on
Paganism)

THE ROWAN EXCHANGE
"A confidential contacts mail forwarding service. The
Rowan Exchange was created to enable Pagans
and Wiccans to have confidential, private and
protected mail contacts with other Pagans and
Wiccans."
Sample copy: $3.00 (U.S. and Canada); $4.00 for
overseas (U.S. funds or I.M.O. only)
The Rowan Exchange
P.O. Box 63
Mt. Horeb, WI 53572

*TGG: INTERNATIONAL JOURNAL OF CRYSTAL
ENLIGHTENMENT*
"A quarterly of spells, runes, Shamanism, contacts,
and more!"
Sample copy: $5.00
TGG
c/o Unicorn Coven
P.O. Box 219
Galveston, IN 46932

UNKNOWN NEWSLETTER
"About various unexplained phenomena, UFOs, and
   Witchcraft."
Sample copy: $2.00
Unknown Newsletter
c/o Luna Ventures
P.O. Box 398
Suisun, CA 94585-0398

THE WINGED CHARIOT
"A newsletter devoted to the Tarot."
Sample copy: $2.00; one year subscription: $10.00
The Winged Chariot
c/o Tracey Hoover
P.O. Box 1718
Milwaukee, WI 53201

THE WITCH'S PAGE
Sample copy: $1.00
The Witch's Page
160 Carriage Lane
Chicago Heights, IL 60411

YGGDRASIL
A "quarterly journal of heathen magick and culture."
Sample copy: $2.00; one year subscription: $6.00
Yggdrasil
537 Jones Street (#165)
San Francisco, CA 94102-2007

Bibliography

Adler, Margot: *Drawing Down the Moon*, Beacon Press, Boston, MA, 1979.

Beyerl, Paul: *The Master Book of Herbalism*, Phoenix Publishing Inc., Custer, WA, 1984.

Bricklin, Mark, executive editor: *The Practical Encyclopedia of Natural Healing*, Rodale Press, Emmaus, PA, 1976.

Buchman, Dian Dincin: *Herbal Medicine*, Gramercy Publishing Company, New York, NY, 1980.

Buckland, Raymond: *Buckland's Complete Book of Witchcraft*. Llewellyn Publications, St. Paul, MN, 1986.

Crowther, Arnold and Patricia: *The Secrets of Ancient Witchcraft*, Citadel Press, Secaucus, NJ, 1974.

Drury, Nevill: *Dictionary of Mysticism and the Occult*, Harper and Row, New York, NY, 1985.

Farrar, Janet and Stewart: *A Witch's Bible Compleat*, Magickal Childe Publishing, Inc., New York, NY, 1984.

Farrar, Janet and Stewart: *The Witches' God*, Phoenix Publishing, Custer, WA, 1989.

Fitch, Ed and Janine Renee: *Magical Rites From the Crystal Well*, Llewellyn Publications, St. Paul, MN, 1984.

Gordon, Lesley: *Green Magic*, Viking Press, New York, NY, 1977.

Hylton, William H., editor: *The Rodale Herb Book*, Rodale Press, Emmaus, PA, 1974.

Leach, Maria and Jerome Fried: *Funk and Wagnalls Standard Dictionary of Folklore, Mythology, and Legend*, Harper & Row, New York, NY, paperback edition 1984.

Lust, John: *The Herb Book*, Bantam Books, New York, NY, 1974.

Morwyn: *Secrets of a Witch's Coven*, Whitford Press, West Chester, PA, 1988.

Slater, Herman, editor: *A Book of Pagan Rituals*, Samuel Weiser, York Beach, ME, 1978.

Index

20, 27, 33, 110
Rood Day, 26 (see also Beltane)
Rowan Exchange (journal), 189
Rowan tree, 42, 156, 168, 174, 175
Rudemas, 26 (see also Beltane)

Sabbats, 15, 17, 24-37, 39, 41, 57,
  64-85, 103; candle colors of, 37;
  gemstones of, 37; incense, 36-37;
  traditional ritual herbs of, 103
Sacred groves, 35, 154-155
Sacred marriage, 57
Saint Patrick, 157
Sakura-No-Miya, 160
Salamanders, 41
Salem, Mass., 20-21
Salt, 42
Samhain, 24, 26, 32-34, 37, 39, 57,
  81-83, 103, 179
Santa Claus, 36
Santeria, 160, 162, 166
Saturn, 96, 97, 106, 107, 170, 174
Saturnalia, 34
Seal of Solomon, 43-44
Second Festival of Harvest, 26 (see
  also Autumn Equinox Sabbat)
Self-Initiation, 46-49
Sin, 14
Solitary Witches, 15, 46
Spirit oil, 144
Spring Equinox Sabbat, 24, 25,
  27-28, 36, 37, 67-69, 103
Summer Solstice Sabbat, 24, 26, 30,
  36, 37, 72-76, 103
Sun God, 27, 28, 36, 69
Swastika symbol, 45
Sycamore tree, 150, 172, 174
Sylphs, 42
Symbols, 42-45

Talismans, 92-93
Telepathic dreams, 177
T.G.G. (journal), 189
Theophrastus, 101
Third Eye, 44, 145
Third Eye Ritual, 56-57
Third Festival of Harvest, 26 (see
  also Samhain)
Thor, 96, 98, 99, 163, 172, 173
Threefold Law, 13
Traditional Pagan foods, 27-32, 34,
  36
Trees, 149-175
Trefoil God, 157
Triangle, 43
Tricken bags, 92
Tricks, 92
Trident, 44, 157

Triformis, 52
Triple Goddess, 10, 28, 43, 44, 52, 81,
  105, 109, 157, 164, 174

Unknown Newsletter, 190

Vampires, 156
Venus, 97, 105, 107, 108, 172, 173
Vernal Equinox, 25, 28 (see also
  Spring Equinox Sabbat)
Virgin Mary, 27, 106-108
Vishnu, 99, 159
Voodoo loas, 144

Walpurgisnacht, 26 (see also
  Beltane)
Wand, 41-42
Warlocks, 14
Wassailing, 36
Wiccan handfasting cakes, 147
Wiccan Rede, 13, 88
Wiccan traditions, 10, 13
Wild-women, 150
Willed imagination, 87
Willow, 42, 151, 155, 168-169, 172, 174
Winged Chariot (journal), 190
Winter Rite, 26 (see also Winter
  Solstice Sabbat)
Winter Solstice Sabbat, 24, 26, 34-37,
  83-85, 103
Wishing cap, 163
Witchcraft trials and executions,
  20-21
Witch Day, 168
Witches' Liberation, 21-23
Witches' sachet, 92
Witch's Page (journal) 190
Woden, 16, 98
World Tree, 152
Wortcunning, 100-136 (see also
  Herbs)

Xolotl, 98, 153

Yarrow love vision spell, 179-180
Yew, 169, 172, 174
Yggdrasil, 152-153
Yggdrasil (journal), 190
Yin and Yang, 17
Yule, 26 (see also Winter Solstice
  Sabbat)
Yule log, 34-35, 84-85, 165

Zeus, 35, 98, 99, 106-108, 154, 172-174
Zodiac (signs of), 43, 104; (herbs of),
  125-136

GERINA DUNWICH was born on December 27, 1959, under the sign of Capricorn with a Taurus rising. She is a Solitary Witch, cat-lover, poet, professional astrologer, witchcraft historian, and student of the occult arts.

She has written many newspaper and magazine articles and is the author of numerous books, including *Candlelight Spells, The Magick of Candleburning, The Concise Lexicon of the Occult* (all available in paperback from Citadel Press), and *Circle of Shadows* (available from Golden Isis Press. See listing in the Pagan periodicals chapter.). She has appeared on radio talk shows across the United States and Canada, and her Goddess-inspired poetry has been published in many Pagan journals and newsletters.

She is a member of the American Biographical Institute Board of Advisors, and is listed in a number of reference works including: *Who's Who in the East, Personalities of America, Who's Who of Emerging Leaders in America*, and *Crossroads: A Who's Who of the Magickal Community.*

Gerina Dunwich currently lives in Southern California, where she edits and publishes *Golden Isis*, a Wiccan literary journal of poetry and Pagan art.